enjoy

new veg with dash

enjoy

nadine abensur

Collins

For my parents and for Noah

First published in 2005 by
Collins, an imprint of
HarperCollinsPublishers
77-85 Fulham Palace Road
Hammersmith
London W6 8JB

The Collins website address is www.collins.co.uk

Collins is a registered trademark of HarperCollins Publishers Ltd

11	10	09	08	07	06	05
7	6	5	4	3	2	1

Text © Nadine Abensur 2005
Main Photography © Ian Wallace 2005

Editor: Jane Middleton
Design: Smith & Gilmour, London
Photographer: Ian Wallace
Food stylist: Julz Beresford
Home economist: Christine Rodrigues

Photographs on pages 55, 93, 147 and 181 by David Young;
photographs on pages 2, 18, 57, 88, 111 and 191 by Marc Gerritsen

A catalogue record for this book is available from the British Library.

ISBN 0-00-720171-0

Colour reproduction by Colourscan, Singapore
Printed and bound by Imago

Contents

Introduction

We left Morocco when I was eight, nearly nine. There were humiliations and excruciating moments, such as the time, a few days into my first week at an English school, when a blond, pink-faced child came to me holding out a pair of white cotton socks. I had come to school in little French sandals, straight from Le Printemps, white and open-toed with sweet fringed details. 'My Mummy says you can have these if you're too poor to buy socks.' I swear these were the first words of English I learned. 'Poor?' I wanted to shout. 'Poor? We had servants and a villa and a life you couldn't even dream of.' I defiantly came to school without socks on for the rest of the summer.

But what could I do about the food? Lunchtime after lunchtime was spent on the stage in front of the whole school because I could not swallow the revolting rice pudding, the lumpy semolina, the nauseating banana custard – to this day I cannot bear to be in the same room as a cooked banana. I cried till the rice pudding ran watery and cold, and was eventually released when the bell rang for class again. I learned to hide food in pockets and handkerchiefs like the most compulsive anorexic.

Home, thank God, was a different story. My mother, who had never needed to cook before, took to the kitchen with some reluctance but great skill. And though she was now a working mother of three, with a big job in Knightsbridge, she brought the cooking of French, only-just-post-colonial Casablanca with her, consulting the few relatives who had made this unlikely migration, sometimes even those in Paris, Washington and Montreal. And it took some doing, finding fennel and pumpkin, artichokes and salsify, celeriac and fresh petits pois, in Richmond-upon-Thames circa 1966.

She made gratins and soufflés, tarts and crêpes (these always in big piles, which she counted out in batches of ten and froze, to thaw over a pan of boiling water when the time came). And for festivals and special occasions, there were day-long preparations of couscous with its seven vegetables, *bstilla* with poussins, tagines with prunes, onions and almonds, *kfita* and *pastelles*, cumin-braised vegetables, and salads of all kinds. My parents were not rich but they had no concept of frugality or economy – not when it came to food (or gorgeous clothes, or much else really).

And nowhere more grandly and magnificently than when they entertained. I recently read an article by a well-known American author in which she questioned the motives for going to great lengths when entertaining. Was it to impress, she wondered, and what did that say? To my parents, this would be an outrageous and incomprehensible line of thought. Very clearly it is to please, to delight, to give – and yes, to do one's best not just to give but to give as much as one is capable of giving.

Our housewarming party (I was eleven by then) was a grand affair and my parents worked at it for days, perhaps weeks. The best solid-silver French cutlery is being used, and the tablecloth, with its garlands of multicoloured sweet peas, exquisitely embroidered for my mother's trousseau by my Great-aunt Phoebe, is laid out, all crisply starched. It is a rarity, the work delightfully and impossibly fine. There are flowers everywhere, crystal glasses as delicate as can be for us children to 'make sing'. There are great silver filigree platters, designed with the entertainment of large numbers in mind. There are numerous apéritifs and canapés, which I have had a hand in assembling. It goes on and on. Someone, an English relative, says it is a lovely spread. Spread? The word jars terribly. My heart sinks a little. Is that how you describe it? I ask myself. This is a banquet and a feast, celebration and ceremony. I look at the guests rather piteously and can't hear the word even now without a slight shudder of horror and disappointment. The word buffet, with its emphasis on the first syllable like shoeshine, has the same effect. I didn't plan a career in food – in fact a part of me is still waiting to go back to my first love, psychology. But the culinary legacy of my childhood had a very long arm and I am still driven to communicate the unique skills and attitudes that were handed down to me. I've done this in various ways over the last twenty years. I ran a vegetarian catering business for eight years, which of course meant organising and cooking for party after party. I treated each one as if it were my very own celebration, my very own feast. I worked till I dropped. When I became food director of the vegetarian restaurant group Cranks, I tried to imbue the food there with a different aesthetic, a new finesse, and then I put it all into my books, hoping again to reach a receptive audience. Now I teach hands-on cookery classes from my home, which overlooks the green hills of northern New South Wales, and I feel in my element. There is a conviviality and bonhomie in the classes that I couldn't have predicted, and an amazing warmth that brings all sorts of different people together and

makes cooking the lively, communal activity it's supposed to be. There is a spirit of co-operation and creativity that everyone loves and responds to. Sometimes people laugh so much they have tears running down their faces. It's just amazing. So you can understand why I frequently teach corporate groups on a 'team-building' exercise, why supper groups have formed as a result of the classes, and why people leave feeling a little less afraid of the kitchen than they were before. At the end of every class we all sit down together at my long table and eat the fruits of our labour – yet another feast!

I'm now in the fortunate and unusual position of writing a book across two continents. I am familiar with the shops and ingredients of both, so I feel as if I've become a sort of go-between, introducing to each the good foods of the other, and making adjustments where necessary. For instance, Turkish bread as it is produced in Australia is delicious – the dough pillowy and light, the crust soft and studded with sesame seeds, a fantastically versatile product. It is available in the UK in areas with sizeable Greek communities but not as readily as in Australia, so I suggest ciabatta as an alternative – that is, until someone picks up the baton and starts to make it in the UK on the same scale as they do in Australia. Asian ingredients are, of course, very easy to get in Australia and I now take them completely for granted. I know they aren't always so easy to find in the UK, so I suggest substituting brown sugar for palm sugar, if necessary, or cinnamon for cassia bark. And, of course, there are everyday ingredients available on both continents that simply have different names – aubergines/eggplants, for example. In the recipes, the Australian terminology follows the English in brackets.

How I Shop

Like everyone who enjoys cooking and eating, I love using fresh produce. I like to know where it has been grown and even who has grown it. It awakens my palate and my enthusiasm for cooking every time.

I haven't specified organic ingredients at every turn in the recipes in this book but I want to say it now, loudly and clearly: organic is best. The Chinese talk of Chi in food – life itself – and this is what I look for when I buy organic food. I simply feel that it has more life in it. It has been grown without the use of chemicals, in ways that aren't harmful to the environment, and some recent studies have shown that it is likely to contain more nutrients than non-organic food.

By contrast, the food that appears perfect in supermarkets can seem dead. This isn't surprising – it's often been picked when underripe, to withstand a long journey, sometimes from the other side of the world, then kept in specially modified storage to extend its shelf life and pumped full of ethylene gas to force the ripening process. Some produce, including apples, pears and citrus fruit, is waxed to enhance its appearance. Then it is overchilled and often overpackaged. It's no wonder it can feel pretty alien.

I know it isn't always possible to buy organic but in both the UK and Australia it is easy to join an organic box scheme and, for a reasonable sum, receive a good selection of whatever happens to be abundant that week. Then there is the amazing growth in farmers' markets, as more and more of us reclaim a vital connection to the food we eat. The produce sold at farmers' markets is not necessarily organic but it will have been grown locally and picked when it is properly ripe and therefore at its peak of flavour. We're back to the question of Chi. And to the possibility that we don't have to rely solely on supermarkets any more, which is good news.

It's an interesting irony how well farmers' markets do in the city, wherever you are in the world. The further we go from Nature, the more we need to seek it out and enjoy it. This is not just a question of being 'worthy'. There is the all-important taste factor. For example, I love my eggs to look and feel as if they've come from a hen (or a duck for that matter), not from a factory, date-stamped and coded, individually washed and unnaturally clean, buffed to within an inch of their life. The difference in taste between an organic egg and a battery-farmed one is so striking that if you have the choice, there is no choice. In organic eggs, the white is generous and firm rather than weak and watery; the yolk is bright, fresh and creamy, not floury and dry; the smell is clean and without the fishiness I'd come to associate with eggs. Organic eggs are the bee's knees.

I may turn my nose up at many shop-bought things these days, but at a farmers' market I'll give everything a go, knowing it's been made by someone who frankly wouldn't bother unless they cared. Really, really cared.

How I Cook

There are a few tricks to good cooking and they come with practice. I'd like to discuss them at the beginning of this book so that you can remember them as you go on. Of course, you might know them like the back of your hand already; you might have been born to them or you might just have a deep, intuitive sense of what is right. You just know when something is done: you look with your eyes and smell with your nose, touch with your fingers and listen with your ears. You enjoy eating – the biggest key – and you have the ability to translate the experience of your taste buds into the actual practice of cooking: the adjustment of heat, the addition of spices, the marriage of ingredients, the all-important timing – all the things that kitchen-bound generations understood instinctively.

We live in a society of buzzwords and glossy pictures, which fail to capture the heart of real food. We've had at least a decade of *al dente* this and that, of vegetables waved over a naked flame in the name of speed and modernity or to make them more photogenic. We've had a glut of 'assembly food', of recipes that barely seem to require our active presence and involvement in the kitchen, and we are in danger of forgetting some fundamentals.

In the recipes in this book, I'll often ask for the food to be very well browned, properly caramelised, allowed to simmer at length. I will practically beg you to cook your vegetables till they are very soft (which never means soggy), aware that for a long time you have been instructed only to steam them so that they retain that apparently desirable crunch. This may be appropriate for a quickly thrown-together stir-fry but it's not right for a tagine or a braise, a casserole or a roast. Neither is it suitable for pulses, which should be so soft that they dissolve when pressed with the tongue against the palate. There is no speeding this up, except by using a pressure cooker. No chickpea, lentil, or any other pulse for that matter should have even the slightest toughness to it. If you are told otherwise, it's wrong and it won't taste good. End of story.

Don't try to apply the rules of Asian cooking to the food of the Middle East, and vice versa. They are very, very different. To give you one example, it's no good treating an aubergine in a Middle Eastern recipe as if it were a carrot in an Asian one. The former needs a copious quantity of hot oil, the latter will work in only a little. One needs to be very soft and browned, the other should have bite. Don't eat a piece of aubergine that looks insipid and half raw. You won't enjoy it so, whatever you do, don't cook it that way.

Slow cooking, the lynchpin of so much Mediterranean and Middle Eastern food, draws out layers of flavour, a depth of taste that you simply will not get by searing things in a hot pan for a minute or so. And get over the fear of oil. In some of these recipes you will have to use oil liberally, but remember that good-quality olive and macadamia oils are fantastically good for you.

Ditto salt. People have often watched me cook in a class, then reproduced the dish exactly so that it looked identical to mine, yet still it lacked roundness. Whenever I probe, I discover fear of salt at the root of this. Of course you don't have to go overboard, but salt brings flavours together in a way that hits the spot. Paradoxically, you may find that you need to eat less when your food is perfectly seasoned than when it's bland. I sometimes find myself chasing after taste, hoping the next mouthful will reveal all. But it doesn't work like that.

Cooking and eating are about sustenance, pleasure, delight and *joie de vivre*. They are about good-quality ingredients, so fresh you can still feel the pulse of life in them. They are about feeding the people you love. It makes sense that you should want your cooking to be as good as possible, that you continually seek inspiration.

Everyone enjoys eating good food and everyone can learn to enjoy cooking it. Do go to people who know their own food well. Try out as many ethnic restaurants as you can, go to hands-on cookery classes, get stuck in, practise, and above all enjoy.

My Basic Recipes

Chermoula

This pungent classic Moroccan sauce, conceived with grilled fish in mind, is fantastic with charred vegetables, with pilafs and couscous, on grilled bread with wilted spinach and a poached egg, or instead of pesto in a Moorish take on bruschetta, with properly charred aubergines (see page 50) the perfect accompaniment. Do taste as you go along when adding the lemon juice. In England I've used 2 whole lemons, small and somewhat devoid of juice, for this. In Australia, it must be said, as little as half an enormous Meyer lemon will do.

a large bunch of coriander, tough
   stalks removed, roughly chopped
a large bunch of parsley, tough stalks
   removed, roughly chopped
6 large garlic cloves, very finely
   chopped
2 tablespoons ground cumin
1 tablespoon sweet paprika
1 teaspoon harissa
1 small bird's eye chilli, finely chopped
juice of ½–2 lemons, to taste
350ml extra virgin olive oil
sea salt

Mix all the ingredients together using a fork, so that the oil and spices make a paste loosened by the lemon juice and rough with herbs and garlic. Or pound the chopped ingredients briefly in a pestle and mortar and then stir in the remaining ingredients.

Pesto

If you are making this with rocket, you might like to replace the pine nuts with almonds or pecan nuts.

30g pine nuts
4 garlic cloves, very finely chopped
a bunch of very fresh basil or rocket
   (about 60g trimmed weight)
2 pinches of sea salt
a pinch of freshly ground black pepper
120ml extra virgin olive oil
40g Parmesan cheese, freshly grated

Grind the pine nuts in a food processor to a mixture of fine and coarser grits, then add the garlic. Blitz for a moment and add the basil and salt and pepper, blitzing again as you slowly pour in the olive oil to make a thick, well-flavoured pesto. Add the cheese and whiz together for a few seconds. Either use immediately or transfer to a jar, pour a protective layer of olive oil on top and seal. The pesto will keep like this in the fridge for up to a month. Use on roasted vegetables, bruschetta, in risotto and, of course, with pasta.

Harissa

Having gone through the ignominious task of making harissa with dried chillies –
think surgical gloves and hour-long removal of seeds – and, worse, having imposed
the torture on willing course participants, I now only ever make my harissa with
fresh chillies. Quick, easy, versatile, it can be kept in the fridge to add to dressings
(a basic vinaigrette is transformed by it), to stir into tagines for a final kick, to serve
with couscous and roasted or charred vegetables, with poached eggs or any other
type of egg for that matter, or even on its own with warm pita, olive oil and dukka.

7 large, bright-red, very fresh chillies
2 tablespoons olive oil
3–4 plump garlic cloves, roughly
    chopped
1 teaspoon coriander seeds
1 teaspoon caraway seeds
1 teaspoon dried mint
1 scant teaspoon ground cumin
1 teaspoon sea salt

Slit the chillies in half and remove the seeds and pith, then chop finely. Put the olive oil,
garlic, coriander and caraway seeds, mint, cumin and salt in a pestle and mortar or a
food processor with a herb chopping attachment and either grind to a paste or pulse
several times. Briefly pound or process with the chopped chilli. Sealed in an airtight
container, the harissa will keep in the fridge for at least 2 weeks.

Dukka

Traditionally dukka is served as a dip for warm pita or broken-up fried tortillas
that have first been dipped briefly in olive oil. You could also add it to roasted or
grilled vegetables, warm wilted spinach or a mustardy, garlicky cauliflower salad.
It's become as essential as salt and pepper on my table.

250g sesame seeds
125g coriander seeds
60g hazelnuts
60g ground cumin
sea salt

Roast the seeds, nuts and cumin separately by placing them in a dry frying pan over
a low heat for a minute or two, until they are lightly browned and their aromas are
released; don't let them become too dark. Pound them together in a pestle and mortar
until finely crushed but not pulverised; it should be a dry mixture rather than a paste.
Season with salt to taste, then store in an airtight container until required.

Ras-al-hanout

Ras-al-hanout is a North African spice mix – traditionally the 'grocer's mix' or literally 'top of the shop'. It is a pot-luck concoction, put together for you by the merchant himself, and can contain as many as 40 different herbs and spices, hailing from the four corners of the world. It demonstrates the sensibility behind Moroccan cooking – the intricate and surprising mix of sweet and savoury, the colours, scents and aromas – and it is always applied with a delicate hand. My father often praised Moroccan cooking for its roundness of flavour. Though hot peppers are used, they rarely dominate. And I often find that, in my own cooking, I use practically immeasurable bits of this and that till I've obtained a taste that refers to its components in only the subtlest of ways.

3–4cm chunk of fresh ginger
8 small, tight dried rosebuds
   (available from Middle Eastern
   and Asian food shops)
5 cloves
½ small cinnamon stick
½ teaspoon ground cumin
½ teaspoon sweet paprika
4cm piece of fresh red chilli,
   deseeded and very finely chopped
⅛ red pepper, chopped

Preheat the oven to 150°C/Gas Mark 2. Peel the ginger, pare it very thinly with a sharp knife and then dry it in the oven for 20–25 minutes. Put it in a pestle and mortar with the rosebuds, spices, chilli and red pepper and pound them together to make a smooth, fragrant paste. Add to dressing (see page 78) or tagines.

Tomato and Olive Salsa

4 small, very red, ripe, sweet
   tomatoes, finely chopped
80g pitted green olives
   (lemon-stuffed ones are great
   for this), finely chopped
a small handful of parsley,
   very finely chopped
2 tablespoons extra virgin olive oil
1 small piece of preserved lemon,
   thinly sliced (optional)
juice of ½ lemon
1 shallot (golden shallot) or
   a small piece of red onion,
   very finely chopped

Simply mix all the ingredients together.

Red Curry Paste

Red curry paste is the one most commonly used in Thai cooking, not merely for curries but for other dishes too. It's worth making twice the quantity, as it keeps in an airtight container in the fridge for up to 3 weeks.

2 teaspoons coriander seeds
1 teaspoon cumin seeds
1 teaspoon white peppercorns
2 star anise
2 cardamom pods
2 cloves
½ teaspoon sea salt
11 large dried red chillies, deseeded, soaked in hot water for 10 minutes, then drained and finely chopped
1 tablespoon finely chopped fresh galangal
2 tablespoons finely chopped lemongrass
1 teaspoon finely chopped coriander root
1 tablespoon finely chopped fresh ginger
1½ teaspoons chopped red turmeric (or ½ teaspoon ground turmeric)
6 tablespoons finely chopped garlic
4 tablespoons finely chopped shallots (golden shallots)
1 teaspoon shrimp paste
1 tablespoon finely shredded kaffir lime leaves, cut from either side of the woody spine

Toast the coriander and cumin seeds, peppercorns, star anise, cardamom and cloves in a dry frying pan over a moderate heat until they are aromatic. Grind to a powder, then pound them in a large mortar and pestle with all the remaining curry paste ingredients except the kaffir lime leaves, adding the dry ingredients first, then the wet ones, and waiting until each ingredient is turned to a paste before adding the next. (You can use a food processor if you're short of time but try at least once using a mortar – it's a much more satisfying experience.) Stir in the lime leaves.

Red Curry and Coconut Sauce

1 tablespoon red curry paste
1 tablespoon desiccated coconut (or freshly grated coconut)
4 tablespoons Greek yoghurt
a little fresh coriander, to garnish

Mix the curry paste, coconut and yoghurt together in a bowl and garnish with the coriander.

Ingredients

Below are some notes on ingredients which may be less familiar, or
where I want to recommend that you use a particular type, or where
there are differences between the UK and Australia.

Argan Oil

Argan oil is unique to Morocco. It has a slightly nutty flavour and comes from the
argan tree, which yields a small fruit a little like an olive. When I was last in England,
I was impressed to find it in Sainsbury's.

Cassia Bark

Cassia bark (see photo on page 21) is from the cassia tree, a member of the *Cinnamomum*
family, and has an intense aroma of cinnamon. The reddish-brown bark comes in large,
wide curls and can be ground to a deep-red powder, slightly sweet, with bitter notes.
I use my big, heavy pestle and mortar to grind it and release the essential oils, which
are warming and energising and said to induce euphoria. I also find that dry-roasting,
as with other spices, releases additional flavour.

Cassia bark is one of the five ingredients of Chinese five-spice powder, the others
being cloves, fennel seeds, star anise and Sichuan pepper.

Add it to pilafs, salad dressings and, of course, to curries.

Fresh Turmeric

Fresh turmeric is most unusual in appearance, like a finger with five little appendages
hanging down from it. It is the root of a plant, *Curcuma longa*, that resembles
ornamental gingers, with flowers that can vary in colour from brightest red to palest
lilac. Asian supermarkets are a good source of the fresh root and it is definitely worth
seeking out in preference to the powdered alternative.

Galangal

Galangal is a hard rhizome with pink shoots, not dissimilar in appearance to ginger,
though it tastes very little like it – despite the often-seen suggestion to substitute ginger
for it in its absence. It is much harder, much hotter and a little bitter. Keep it in the
fridge, submerged in a bowl of water. It is an essential ingredient in Thai curries.

Kaffir Limes

A weird thing, the kaffir lime, all gnarled and convoluted peel, yielding little juice
but an incredible flavour. The peel is thinly pared or zested to use in curries. The leaves,
which are easier to buy, also carry the distinctive aroma and are usually cut into thin
strips from either side of the fibrous spine.

Lemons

I use organic lemons when I can, though I found out recently that organic ones are not
necessarily unwaxed. Now I buy unwaxed lemons when I particularly need to use the zest.

Lemongrass

This is a perennial grass native to South Asia and widely used in its cooking. Like other lemon-scented ingredients, it lends itself extremely well to both sweet and savoury uses. It is better known for its role in savoury things, but left to infuse in custards it imparts a delicious and delicate afternote. Use only the white, bulbous part, discarding the green part and the tough, outer leaves. When using lemongrass in salads, always slice it as thinly as possible with the sharpest knife you have. Otherwise, split the stem down the middle and bash with the back of a knife to release the fragrant, lemony perfume. I recommend that you freeze any lemongrass sticks you are not using straight away, the green part removed, in sealed plastic bags. Use them, bashed to release their perfume, the next time you make a Thai-inspired curry.

Lemon Myrtle

From trees that grow up to 6 metres high, glossy, dark-green lemon myrtle leaves can be used fresh in curries or dried and pounded to a powder. They have fresh, lemony, eucalyptus notes and some varieties also have a pronounced aniseed flavour. On my visit to Brookfarm (see below) I discovered another of lemon myrtle's properties: it keeps the dreaded mozzies away. You'll be pleased to know that you can now buy the powdered form in the UK from Harvey Nichols stores, or you can order it via the internet on www.herbies.com.au

Macadamia Oil

Brookfarm's organic macadamia oil is the pride and joy of the Byronshire. It is an extremely fine thing, and when you speak to Martin and Pam Brook you can see why: their palpable passion and their search for perfection; the obvious pride in their superior nut, which is kept disease free through the use of copper; the way in which they have succeeded in reducing to almost zero the ravages caused by rats – not through trapping but by the introduction, Harry Potter style, of owls. And the way that, by encouraging the proliferation of the rainforest that surrounds the trees, they are able to keep pest control to a minimum. They grow 4,500 trees on 90 acres of prime, lipstick-red volcanic soil.

Brookfarm macadamia oil has found a special spot in my kitchen. It is a monounsaturated oil with more health claims than olive oil, a higher heating point and a milder, less pervasive flavour. Making the most of an indigenous product that lends itself to organic production seems such an obvious step that I don't see why Australia and macadamia oil should be any less intimately associated than Italy and olive oil, nor any less respected. And in my book, it certainly beats the horribly pervasive use of (genetically modified) canola (rapeseed) oil.

However, that is only part of the story. Martin and Pam were among the first to see beyond the apparently intractable nut – its shell requires a special vice-like nut cracker – and spent two years developing their range of fine oils, mueslis and spiced nuts. These are now exported world wide, with particular success in the UK, where the lemon-myrtle-infused macadamia oil was a gold-medal winner at the 2004 Great Taste Awards. It is a delicate oil that no kitchen should be without.

Potatoes

For potato salads and braises, I use the smallest, waxiest, yellow-fleshed new potatoes I can find, so that they maintain their shape even when very tender. In Australia Kipfler potatoes – finger-sized, knobbly ones with rich, sweet flesh – work well but there are others the further south you go (for example, in Victoria and Tasmania) that are as good as any of the fabulous French potatoes such as La Ratte.

Shallots (Golden Shallots)

For reasons I haven't delved into, what the French call echalotes, the English call shallots and the Australians call golden shallots. To complicate matters further, spring onions are known in Australia as shallots.

Shiitake Mushrooms

Always a great fan, I seem to have used shiitake mushrooms more than ever before in this book. It's their silky, velvety texture that I find so appealing, plus their ability to soak up both Asian and Western flavours, especially red wine and brandy. Fresh shiitake are now easy to find in supermarkets but the dried version makes a suitable alternative. If using dried mushrooms, soak them in boiling water for about 20 minutes before use.

Star Anise

A flowering bush with pretty white petals and yellow stamens, this is quite possibly the most beautiful of all spices. Star anise is the dark reddish-brown, eight-pointed pod with glossy seeds – the glossier the seeds, the fresher the spice. It has sweet, pungent, liquorice notes. Common in the cooking of Thailand, Vietnam and Indonesia, it hails originally from South China. It can be added to pilafs, is surprisingly good in creamy sauces and fantastic in soups and dressings. It can be ground to a powder, which I then put through a sieve to remove the debris.

Tamarind

The long, brown pods of a tropical tree, this is a major source of sourness in Asian and Middle Eastern cooking. Packs of pressed pods, which need soaking and straining, are a common way to use tamarind. However, they are messy and laborious, so I always buy the ready-made tamarind paste.

Wattle Seeds

Despite the fact that wattle seeds are not yet grown on a commercial scale, they are already exported to America, the UK and other countries. Roasting and grinding the seeds brings out the flavour, which many compare to coffee. Use them in pastries, breads and ice cream. The acacia trees they come from flourish in the arid conditions of large parts of Australia and this has made them an invaluable aid in developing countries with impoverished soil.

Worcestershire Sauce and Fish Sauce

I thought long and hard about whether to include these in my recipes and finally succumbed a couple of times. They are, of course, not vegetarian and they can be replaced with a vegetarian alternative or light soy sauce without detrimental effect.

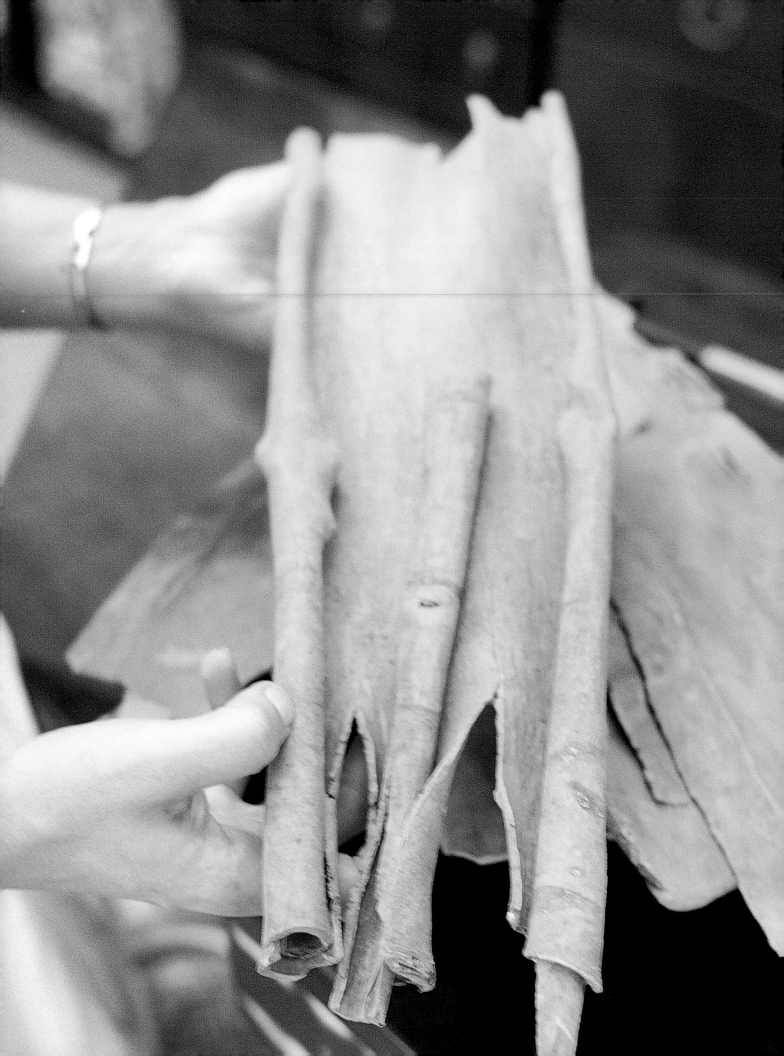

Breakfast in Bed

We all know that breakfast is supposed to be the most important meal of the day, yet very often we snatch a cup of coffee at 7am and a Mars Bar at 11. So the breakfast (or you can call it brunch) in bed bit is about making at least a weekend ritual of this much abused meal. And making it last as long as possible. The bed is optional.

I watch despairingly as someone spreads margarine and sugar-free jam on low-fat crackers. Surely an apple would be better, or a whole plateful of fruit for that matter, with some very good yoghurt and a drizzle of maple syrup. It's not exactly rocket science.

I was brought up by highly organised Virgoan parents, who set the table for breakfast the night before. There was always a light, spongy orange or lemon cake, *petits pains au chocolat*, toast and all the trimmings, a plate of cheese, a bowl of fruit. Sometimes at weekends, there was *pain perdu* (eggy bread) or, as a treat, Moroccan *beignets*. Once in a blue moon we had the full English blow-out breakfast. Years of rebellion later, I've come back to the (breakfast) table and I love it. It's a good way to start the day. Sweet or savoury first thing is a very personal choice (what's wrong with a bit of both?) but I hope that, by gleaning a little from everywhere, I've covered all bases in this chapter and introduced you to ideas you might not otherwise have considered.

$4·50 DOZ

HAWKPAK SU 6

Eggs Florentine with Lemon Myrtle Hollandaise on Potato Rösti

Of course, you could serve this on thick slabs of sourdough bread, butter and all, but I wanted to include a good recipe for rösti that you can use on other occasions, and this quintessential brunch is a good place to do it. If truth be known, though, I rarely like to start the day loaded with carbs, so I'm more likely to eat just the egg, on top of a huge pile of spinach – a whole bag of it, gently wilted – hence the leeway in the spinach quantity below. The recipe includes the still not universally known way to poach an egg, so we can all turn them out in perfect bistro fashion.

SERVES 4

4–8 large, very fresh eggs
1 tablespoon white wine vinegar
2–4 bags of baby spinach
a knob of butter
a pinch of freshly grated nutmeg
sea salt and freshly ground
    black pepper

For the rösti:

3 large, all-purpose potatoes,
    peeled and cut into chunks
60g butter, melted
light olive oil for shallow-frying

For the hollandaise sauce:

180g unsalted butter
4 large egg yolks
1 tablespoon ground lemon myrtle
    (or 1½ tablespoons lemon juice)
a pinch of salt
ground white pepper (optional)

First make the potato rösti. Parboil the potatoes in lightly salted water for 5 minutes, then drain and leave to cool slightly. Grate them into a bowl and mix in the butter and some salt and pepper (you can, at this stage, add other things if you like, such as fried onion, toasted flaked almonds, goat's cheese, snipped chives and other herbs). Heat a film of olive oil in a blini pan, then fill it two-thirds full with the potato mixture. Fry until golden and crisp on both sides and tender on the inside. Repeat with the remaining mixture to make 4 rösti altogether. Keep them warm in a low oven while you prepare the eggs, sauce and spinach.

First poach the eggs. Have a small pan of lightly salted simmering water at the ready, or a deep frying pan, with at least 10cm of water in it. Crack an egg into a saucer. Add the white wine vinegar to the simmering water and stir it furiously to create a little whirlpool in the centre of the pan. Drop the egg into the middle of the cyclone and watch as the egg white spins and arranges itself around the yolk. After 3–4 minutes, remove the egg from the water with a slotted spoon and place on sheets of absorbent kitchen paper. Repeat with the remaining eggs. Just before you are ready to serve, you can lower the eggs back into the water a couple at a time, sitting on a spider (a flat, wire-meshed sieve), just to warm them through – a minute will do. Trim off any straggly tendrils of egg white, drain again and serve.

To make the hollandaise sauce, gently melt the butter in a pan. Whiz the egg yolks in a blender for 30 seconds or simply whisk well by hand. Transfer them to a bowl and place it over a pan of simmering water, making sure the water doesn't touch the base of the bowl. Add the lemon myrtle – I sift it in through a tea strainer to stop it going lumpy – or lemon juice and mix well, then slowly drizzle the butter into the eggs a little at a time, whisking all the time with a balloon whisk. When the butter is all incorporated, you should have a bowl of thick, creamy hollandaise. Add a little salt to taste and a touch of white pepper if you wish.

Put the spinach in a pan with the knob of butter, cover and leave over a gentle heat until wilted. Season with the nutmeg and some sea salt and black pepper. Serve the rösti topped with an egg or two, plus a mound of spinach and a coating of Hollandaise.

Buttermilk Pancakes with Caramelised Apples and Brandy Caramel Sauce

I like to serve these for breakfast, brunch or afternoon tea (in which case, think cream or ice cream) to replace my usual crêpes, but not for dessert, where they strike me as just too rich.

If you make the pancakes in a blini pan they don't look huge, but if you consider that when I tried them a different way, each serving made at least 8 little pancakes – or *poffertjes* (the Dutch word for them) – you'll see that one per person is plenty. A couple who do the rounds of the North Coast markets, in New South Wales, in their catering van sell *poffertjes* in mounds on paper plates, piled high with whipped cream and oodles of maple syrup. There are always queues.

It's worth noting that you can freeze the cooled pancakes layered with baking parchment or foil, then place them in a steamer over boiling water to bring them back to life.

MAKES 8 PANCAKES OR
ABOUT 80 POFFERTJES
250g plain flour
a pinch of salt
1 tablespoon baking powder
1 teaspoon bicarbonate of soda
100g caster sugar
4 eggs, separated
500ml buttermilk
sunflower oil for frying
Greek yoghurt and finely chopped
  toasted pecan nuts, to serve

For the caramelised apples:
300g caster sugar
125g unsalted butter
4–5 large apples (I use Pink Ladies),
  peeled, cored and sliced

For the caramel sauce:
250g caster sugar
60ml water
80ml brandy (or about two-thirds
  brandy and one-third red wine)
60ml pouring cream

It's easiest to start by cooking the apples and making the caramel sauce. You can gently reheat both just before serving.

For the apples, put the sugar and butter in a large saucepan or frying pan and cook over a careful heat until golden. Add the apple slices – splutter and sizzle is part of the fun – and cook until they are tender, almost translucent, and oozing with caramel (you may decide that this is enough decadence and forego the caramel sauce!). Remove from the heat and set aside.

For the caramel sauce, combine the sugar and water in a small, heavy-based saucepan and stir over a low heat until the sugar has dissolved. Raise the heat and boil, without stirring, until the syrup turns a dark caramel colour. Immediately remove from the heat and, very carefully and with a step back, as it will spit rather dramatically, stir in the brandy. Return the pan to a low heat and stir until smooth, then add the cream and bring back to the boil. Remove from the heat and set aside while you make the pancakes. (Stored in the fridge in a sealed jar, this sauce lasts for ages.)

To make the pancakes, sift the flour, salt, baking powder and bicarbonate of soda into a large bowl and stir in the caster sugar. Lightly whisk the egg yolks in a separate bowl, then slowly pour in the buttermilk and continue to whisk gently – I do all this with a hand whisk – until well amalgamated. Make a well in the centre of the dry ingredients and add the buttermilk mixture. Mix well, by bringing the dry ingredients into the wet a little at a time, until smooth and lump free. Whisk the egg whites in a separate bowl until they form stiff peaks, then slide them out of the bowl with a rubber spatula and gently fold them into the pancake mixture.

If you are using a blini pan – two if you can, to make easier work of this (they're cheap and worth investing in) – lightly dip a piece of crumpled kitchen paper into a saucer of sunflower oil, which you must have by your side. Wipe the pan with it and heat over a moderate heat. Do this before cooking each pancake. Fill the blini pan three-quarters full with the pancake mixture and leave until bubbles appear on the surface –

about 1½–2 minutes should do it. Then turn the pancake over carefully, using a palette knife or fish slice, and cook the other side. The pancakes should be golden brown, cooked right through but still light and fluffy. Transfer to a plate, cover lightly with foil and keep in a warm oven while you cook the remaining pancakes.

If you are making the smaller *proffitjes*, heat a little oil in a large frying pan and drop tablespoonfuls of the mixture into it. They will immediately spread into little round pancakes, which you can help along with the back of a spoon, making them no bigger than 5–6 cm in diameter. These cook quite quickly and will keep you on your toes.

Have warmed plates at the ready. Place 1 large or 8–10 little pancakes on each plate with a mound of richly caramelised apple slices, a generous swirl – make that a pool – of caramel sauce and a dollop of Greek yoghurt (at last, a semblance of sanity!). Stop the world and eat without delay, a smattering of chopped pecans on top.

27 Breakfast in Bed

Blueberry Friands with Warm Blueberries

No cookbook from Australia would be complete without these. It is my fervent hope that they will make it on to the shelves of British coffee bars and cake shops everywhere, the way they do here. And I hope it will be this version, light and moist and eaten still warm or even just warmed. They knock the socks off muffins any day. You can store them in a sealed plastic bag in the fridge for several days, where they keep surprisingly fresh, then reheat them, lightly wrapped in foil.

MAKES 8

200g icing sugar
50g plain flour
130g ground almonds (almond meal)
6 egg whites
grated zest of 1 lemon
170g unsalted butter, melted and cooled, plus a little melted butter for greasing
2 punnets (about 300g) blueberries
2 teaspoons caster sugar
crème fraîche, Greek yoghurt, double cream or vanilla ice cream, to serve

Preheat the oven to 200°C/Gas Mark 6. Brush 8 oval friand moulds (or a muffin tin) with melted butter and dust with flour, shaking out any excess.

Sift the icing sugar and flour into a bowl and stir in the ground almonds (almond meal). In a separate bowl, beat the egg whites to soft peaks. Gently fold them into the dry ingredients. Add the lemon zest and then fold in the cooled melted butter.

Fill each friand mould or muffin cup three-quarters full with the mixture and put 3–4 blueberries on top of each one, so that they are lightly embedded but still visible. Bake for 20 minutes or until the friands spring back when touched.

Meanwhile, place the rest of the blueberries in a small pan with the caster sugar. Crush a few of them with the back of a fork, bring to the boil and simmer until quite syrupy.

Place a warm friand in the centre of each plate with a good spoonful of warm blueberries on top and some crème fraîche, Greek yoghurt, double cream or vanilla ice cream.

Mofleta

I have a fond nostalgia for these simple, bready pancakes, and badgered my mother, friends and family for the recipe for years ('It's nothing, darling,' my mother would say, 'just a simple bread dough …'). The Mimouna is a singularly Jewish Moroccan tradition to celebrate the last day of Passover, where the dietary restrictions of the previous 8 days (no leaven of any kind) are lifted. It's a child's idea of heaven – only sweet things are served. There were fancier things by far than mofleta but I always adored these, served oozing with butter and honey. Now, as a seasoned tradition breaker, I suggest serving them for breakfast.

MAKES 10
1 teaspoon dried yeast
a pinch of sugar
about 125ml warm water
250g strong white bread flour
½ teaspoon salt
2 tablespoons olive oil, plus a little
    extra for frying
butter and honey, to serve

Dissolve the yeast with the sugar in about half the water and set aside for about 10 minutes, until it froths. Put the flour, salt and a tablespoon of the olive oil in a large bowl and mix well. Add the yeast mixture and enough of the remaining water for the dough to form a soft ball.

Knead the dough on a lightly floured surface for about 10 minutes, until smooth and elastic. Return it to the bowl and pour the remaining tablespoon of oil over it, rolling it in the bowl till it is oiled and glossy all over. Cover with a tea towel or cling film and leave in a warm place for about 1½ hours, until doubled in size.

Divide the dough into 10 pieces and roll them out as thinly as possible on an oiled work surface. Then pull and stretch them to make them even thinner. Carefully lower one of the dough rounds into a lightly oiled frying pan set over a medium heat and cook for about 2 minutes, until lightly coloured underneath. Turn over and cook the other side for about a minute, then remove from the pan. Repeat with the remaining dough. To keep the mofleta soft and pliable, cover them with a cloth, placing each new one under the previous one. They quickly go hard as they cool, so precautions are necessary. You can reheat them in the oven, if necessary, as long as you wrap them in foil first, but eat them warm you must, copiously buttered and honeyed.

Medjool Dates with Toasted Almonds, Feta and Rose Petals

My childhood accompaniment to this was fresh walnuts rather than almonds, the flesh tender, sweet and white, the skin fine and easy to peel. Toasted almonds make a lovely alternative, and toasted pecans would be gorgeous, too. You can glaze them with a little of the orange blossom syrup, if you like, poured hot over the hot nuts.

As for the feta, all you need is a good, fat chunk of it – I neaten it up with a very sharp knife but you could do the opposite and break it up roughly. The scattering of a few dried rose petals on top and a drizzle of the orange blossom syrup confirms it in its Middle Eastern place, despite using the milder, Danish feta.

SERVES 6–8

60g blanced almonds, slivered
18–24 Medjool dates
150g–180g Danish feta cheese
1 tablespoon Orange Blossom Syrup
    (see 31)
a few dried rose petals, if available

Toast the almonds in a large, dry, frying pan over a gentle heat for about 8 minutes, until pale gold. Arrange the dates on a plate, pyramid like, with the toasted almonds scattered over them. Put the chunk of feta on a separate plate and drizzle the orange blossom syrup over it, then add a scattering of dried rose petals, if using.

Serve with the shortbread biscuits on page 173, replacing the lemon myrtle with the finely grated zest of 1 orange and a few drops of orange oil, if available.

Mascarpone-stuffed Figs in Orange Blossom Syrup

This is one of my dream breakfasts. I've even converted my blokey man (for which read Antipodean Neanderthal – his words!) to it. Drier figs will need longer cooking to soften them up. You can cut corners by using the glossy, semi-dried ones that come in vacuum-packed foil-lined bags.

SERVES 6–8

20–24 dried Turkish figs
250g mascarpone cheese
1 tablespoon icing sugar
1 tablespoon orange blossom water

For the orange blossom syrup:
225ml orange juice
225ml water
225g caster sugar
4 cardamom pods, crushed
3–4 black peppercorns
¾ teaspoon orange blossom water
a sprig of coriander
a dash of lemon juice

Put the orange juice and water in a pan and add the figs. Bring to the boil and simmer for 3–4 minutes, then remove the figs from the pan and set aside. Add the sugar, cardamom pods and black peppercorns to the pan and stir over a low heat to dissolve the sugar. Return to the boil and simmer, without stirring, until syrupy. Then return the figs to the pan for a couple of minutes with the orange blossom water, coriander sprig and lemon juice.

Lift the figs out and allow them to cool completely. Mix together the mascarpone, icing sugar and orange blossom water and put them in a piping bag fitted with a nozzle pointy enough to pierce the figs easily. Fill each fig so it balloons out, almost fit to burst – a little of the filling gently oozing out will tempt all the more. Transfer to a large bowl or cake stand and pour the cooled syrup over. Serve in long-stemmed cocktail glasses with a little of the syrup drizzled over.

Black Rice Pudding with Coconut Cream and Mango

A favourite breakfast at home, this recipe was given to me by my friend Lesley, who co-owns Red Ginger, a gorgeous Asian food and homewares emporium in Byron Bay. Lesley is one of the most effortlessly elegant women I know and this rice pudding, traditional though it is, bears her hallmark.

SERVES 4–6

200g black rice
100g palm sugar
about 1 litre water
a pinch of salt
seeds from 4 cardamom pods,
    or 4 pandanus leaves
grated zest of 1 lemon or lime
300ml coconut cream
3 ripe mangoes, peeled, stoned
    and neatly sliced

Put the rice, sugar, water, salt and cardamom or pandanus leaves in a large pan and bring to the boil. Reduce the heat right down to a whisper, cover with a lid and let the rice simmer away for 45 minutes, stirring regularly. Then turn the heat up and, stirring continuously, cook for another 15 minutes at least, until it's a lovely, sloppy, creamy mixture with separate grains. Stir in the lemon or lime zest and transfer to serving bowls. Top with the coconut cream and the mango, sliced out of the 2 plump, juicy cheeks that you have cut from either side of the stone.

An Israeli Breakfast Platter

As someone who finds breakfast the hardest meal of the day – I never know whether to go for savoury or sweet, and carbohydrate in the morning seems to disagree – I consider this a marvellous way to start the day and I'm sure that any dietician would approve.

In my teens I spent several weeks on a kibbutz. My job was picking pears and sorting them according to size, from the crack of dawn until lunchtime, with a break at 9 o'clock for a breakfast of the fruit and vegetables we had picked. I'd never seen anything like it. Piles of tomatoes, red peppers (capsicums), cucumbers, spring onions (shallots), olives, the best cottage cheese I have ever tasted, soft and sweet with huge curds, simple cheeses, hard-boiled eggs, houmous, nuts in their shells, fresh fruit, including dates and watermelon, and fresh juices. Home-made bread and fruit compotes. You should read Claudia Roden's account of kibbutz food in *The Book of Jewish Food* (Viking, 1997).

And another idea with an aesthetic equally different from the Western norm is the Japanese breakfast of miso and vegetable broth, silken tofu, softened arame seaweed, pickled vegetables and steamed rice. Again, it's easy to stomach first thing in the morning. Because there are so many visitors from Japan to the Gold Coast, many of the hotels serve this for breakfast as a matter of course. These are all habits I have introduced into my kitchen and slowly, slowly to the people around me.

Polenta and Ricotta Cake with Mango, Passion Fruit Syrup and Lime Mascarpone

A light-textured cake that you could make with Greek yoghurt instead of the ricotta, if you prefer – or, indeed, a mix of the two, which is what I often end up doing. The passion fruit syrup makes a dessert of this but it's also good as a breakfast or afternoon tea sort of cake. An average passion fruit yields a mere 2 teaspoons of juice, so although passion fruit grow prolifically in Australia and are very cheap (the equivalent of about 3 pence each), I know 25 passion fruit can seem an exorbitant luxury in the UK. So I have suggested mango juice as an alternative, as it is a more accessible option despite its equally distant origins.

The mango topping is especially abundant, not just sparsely placed slices but more of a generous heap.

SERVES 8–10

100g polenta (not the
quick-cook variety)
300g ricotta cheese
grated zest of 1 orange
grated zest of 1 lemon
grated zest of 1 lime
120g softened unsalted butter
220g caster sugar
3 eggs
200g self-raising flour
½ teaspoon bicarbonate of soda
1–2 mangoes, peeled, stoned and
cut into smallish cubes

For the topping:
50g butter
2 tablespoons caster sugar
3–4 ripe but firm mangoes,
peeled, stoned and sliced
juice of 1 orange
juice of 1 lemon
500ml orange or mango juice

For the passion fruit syrup:
300g caster sugar
100ml water
250ml strained passion fruit juice
or mango juice
the pulp of 6 passion fruit

For the lime mascarpone:
grated zest of 1 lime
200g mascarpone cheese
2 teaspoons icing sugar (optional)

Preheat the oven to 180°C/Gas Mark 4. Line a round 23cm springform cake tin with baking parchment. Combine the polenta, ricotta and citrus zest in a bowl and set aside for about an hour, so the polenta starts to soften.

Beat the butter and sugar together until pale. Beat in the eggs one at a time, making sure that each is well amalgamated. Sift the flour and bicarbonate of soda together and fold them in gently. Then fold in the ricotta and polenta mixture and finally the chopped mango. Pour the mixture into the cake tin and bake for 45 minutes or until a skewer inserted in the centre comes out clean. Remove from the oven, leave to cool in the tin for 10 minutes, then turn out on to a wire rack to cool completely.

Meanwhile, make the topping. Melt the butter and sugar in a large frying pan over a very gentle heat without stirring at all, at most moving the pan around very gently. Add the mango slices and all the juice and simmer for 8–10 minutes, until the juice is almost completely reduced and the mango soft and gently caramelised. Remove from the heat and set aside.

To make the syrup, put the sugar and water in a heavy-based pan and heat gently, stirring occasionally, until the sugar has melted. Raise the heat and bring to the boil, then add the passion fruit or mango juice. Boil for about 10 minutes, until reduced and thickened, then remove from the heat and stir in the passion fruit pulp. Serve warm or cold and store any remaining syrup in the fridge.

Finally stir the lime zest into the mascarpone cheese, with the sugar if using. You can soften the lime zest first in the same pan as the passion fruit syrup if you like, lifting it out after a minute or so.

Arrange the mango slices over the cake – there should be enough for a couple of layers – and serve with the lime mascarpone and passion fruit syrup by the side.

Pineapple and Ginger Punch

This year my lovely friend Elizabeth made us her grandmother's special Christmas drink. Later, I made it myself with juice extracted from 2 fresh pineapples. They cost about 2 dollars each where I live, so you can see why. It's very similar to something we used to make at Cranks and sell by the gallon, but even though I made up the recipe there in the first place I couldn't for the life of me remember quite how it went. Elizabeth turned up with the ingredients, so it all worked out.

MAKES 3 LITRES
1 litre pineapple juice, freshly juiced
   if possible
1 litre ginger ale
1 litre sparkling mineral water
a good handful of mint, roughly
   chopped
a fat knob of fresh ginger, peeled
   and finely shredded or grated,
   then squeezed to extract the juice
juice and grated zest of 1 lime
ice

Mix everything together well in a large bowl or jug and drink while it is still very bubbly.

Silken Tofu and Mango Smoothie

I love this in the mornings but sometimes when the recipe testing has got out of hand – nothing but cake for a week – I like to replace lunch with it too. In Australia, where they know about these things, you can go into a supermarket and find about 15 types of tofu and no one turns their nose up at it. The silken tofu really is like silk, delicate and soothing. In the UK you might have to go to a healthfood shop or an Asian one for the best. By the way, this is a fantastic way of making sure you eat plenty of protein.

Use chilled ingredients to make the smoothie. Replace some of the mango with ripe peaches, if you like. A few blueberries or a couple of strawberries whizzed in also make a treat.

SERVES 6
4 medium-sized ripe mangoes
400ml fruit juice, preferably apple
   and mango
400g silken tofu

Cut a thick slice off each mango from either side of the stone and scoop out the flesh. Peel the rest of the mango and scrape off as much flesh from the stone as you can. Put in a blender with the fruit juice and tofu and blitz until very smooth. Serve at once.

Lime, Lemongrass, Maple Syrup and Chilli Toddy

This is a two-in-one recipe, including not just the toddy but the cordial basis
of an ice-cold drink with sparkling mineral water. If you're a honey person, which
I'm not, you could replace the maple syrup with it. Maple syrup, however, has
a significantly lower glycaemic index then honey, which is as high as sugar so
perhaps not the best thing to kickstart the day. Having said that, I can occasionally
be tempted by the complex Tasmanian Leatherwood honey or a lemon myrtle
honey, both of which would work here.

MAKES ABOUT 600ML
150g fresh ginger, finely grated
2 limes, sliced
3 lemongrass sticks, smashed
1 litre filtered water
350ml maple syrup
a small piece of red chilli,
   finely chopped, or lime wedges
   and a couple of sprigs of mint,
   to serve

Place the grated ginger, lime slices, smashed lemongrass sticks and water in a pan
and bring to the boil. Simmer, partly covered, for 45 minutes, then remove from the
heat and add the maple syrup. Leave to cool and pour into a sterilised bottle.

To make the toddy, top up with a roughly equal amout of boiling water and add the
chilli. Alternatively, dilute the cordial with sparkling mineral water (the ratio of 1:4 seems
to work best here) and serve over ice, with lime wedges and sprigs of mint.

Lemongrass and Rosebud Infusion

My favourite shop, Red Ginger (see photo on page 2), the Asian food emporium in Byron Bay, sells a mix they make up themselves consisting only of dried lemongrass and tiny, pert, deep red, highly scented rosebuds.

I use fresh lemongrass with the rosebuds to make my own infusion. For each cup or glassful, you need 1 stick of lemongrass, white part only, very finely chopped, and 7–8 dried rosebuds. Pour over boiling water and leave to infuse for a few minutes, then add 2 or 3 more rosebuds and drink at once. You can sweeten with a touch of honey or soft brown sugar, if you like. And you can place a stick of trimmed lemongrass in each glass to stir.

On the Barbecue

I'd like to propose the outrageous idea of an all-vegetable barbecue. The only reason that it's hard to imagine is because the veggies are usually reserved until last or squashed into a corner, served undercooked and underdressed as a barely considered afterthought. As you can imagine, this distresses me – all that wasted potential. For a start, there's all the gorgeous colours and things that just naturally go well together. Aubergines (eggplants), courgettes (zucchini) and peppers (capsicums) are age-old partners that respond fantastically to the Barbecue treatment. Don't limit yourself to the recipes here, though. Experiment, play around, enjoy.

A few tips. Have as many sauces, dips, marinades, relishes and jams at your disposal as you can. And remember that vegetables need oil, spices and seasonings to bring out the best in them. They can be marinated for an hour or more before cooking – even overnight is good. They can also be bashed and pounded while they're on the grill to soften them and speed up the cooking time. They can be subjected to extremes of temperature – though having said that, unless you feel completely comfortable around high heat, it's best to work over a medium heat, at least to begin with, and to keep turning the vegetables over.

I grew up in Casablanca, where street vendors stood over old oil barrels filled with glowing coals. They'd grill the corn until practically black, then dip it in heavily salted water. Butter was not an option. The corn didn't have the succulent sweetness that it does now but we children absolutely loved it. I remember many a time sitting in the back of the car while my parents completed their shopping, kept happy by a piping-hot cob, the black coming off on my fingers. I didn't eat a corn on the cob like that for another 30 years, until I went to Jamaica. Now that I live in Australia, I'm making up for lost time.

Good Things to add to your Barbecue

- Juicy lemons cut into quarters or sixths, depending on size, basted very lightly with olive oil and even a pinch of sugar if you like, and placed on the grill for 6 minutes on each side, until completely tender and well charred. You can eat both flesh and skin.
- Instant polenta, made according to the instructions on the packet, spread out in a square cake tin and left to cool and set. Then cut it into triangles, baste with a little olive oil and grill on the hot plate of the barbecue over a medium heat for 2 minutes on each side.
- Thick slices of sourdough bread (or baguette), spread with garlic butter and toasted on the grill.

Tofu Steaks Marinated in Ume Su and a Host of Other Things

The method below is the quick way. For an even better result, cook the marinated
tofu in a frying pan with the marinade for 10–15 minutes over a very high heat (do keep
an eye on it), until the marinade has evaporated and the tofu is very brown, sticky and
caramelised. Only then briefly throw it on to the grill to char and striate both sides.

SERVES 3–6

300g firm tofu, cut into 6 thick slices,
    scored diagonally all over

For the marinade:
1 tablespoon ume su (plum vinegar)
1 tablespoon Chinese rice wine
2 tablespoons water
1 tablespoon olive oil
2 tablespoons tamari
a knob of fresh ginger, grated
1 garlic clove, finely chopped
1 tablespoon maple syrup
1 tablespoon sweet chilli sauce

Put all the marinade ingredients into a dish large enough to take the slices of tofu
lying flat, so each slice can absorb the marinade. Add the tofu and leave to marinate
for at least 20 minutes, even overnight if you have the foresight to do so.

Place the tofu on the hot barbecue plate and cook for 5 minutes, pouring on about
half the marinade, a little at a time, and turning the tofu once. Transfer to the grill side
of the barbecue and give the slices a final 30 seconds on each. Transfer to a plate and
pour the remaining marinade over.

Aubergine Stacks with Mozzarella

I think these became a bit of a cliché for a while but that doesn't stop them being
very good to eat and to look at. You can sandwich the slices of aubergine with all
manner of things – houmous, pesto, grilled and peeled red peppers. Anything
Mediterranean, Moorish or Middle Eastern works well.

SERVES 6

1 aubergine (eggplant), long enough
    to slice into 12
2 large tomatoes, 1 thickly sliced,
    1 roughly chopped
2–3 tablespoons olive oil
a dash of Tabasco sauce
6 thick slices of mozzarella cheese
3 tablespoons pesto (see page 12)
sea salt
a few small basil leaves, to garnish

Brush the aubergine (eggplant) and tomato slices with the olive oil and Tabasco and
sprinkle with salt. Grill the aubergine (eggplant) over a medium heat for 5–6 minutes
on each side. Add the tomatoes and grill for a minute on each side. Remove from the
heat and make into stacks with a slice of mozzarella, a slice of tomato and ½ tablespoon
of pesto between 2 slices of aubergine (eggplant). Return to the barbecue for a minute
on each side, just so the mozzarella can melt. Meanwhile, quickly stir the chopped
tomato on the hot plate of the barbecue, if you have one, then remove. Garnish the
stacks with basil leaves and the chopped tomato and serve.

Sweet Potatoes with Asparagus and Pesto

I often make a salad of these three ingredients, roasting the sweet potatoes till they're prettily browned and tender. The charring over a barbecue is just going a step further. I add goat's cheese or very well marinated and fried tofu, with slivers of sunblush (semi-dried) tomatoes, both of which you could also include here. Pesto is obviously not the only option either. Try extra virgin olive oil, balsamic vinegar and dukka (see page 13) as an alternative. Or any other dressing in the book.

SERVES 4
4 small sweet potatoes,
    preferably thin ones
2 bunches (about 450g) asparagus –
    quite thick spears are best, given
    the vicious treatment
2 ripe tomatoes, cut in half

For the marinade:
2 tablespoons olive oil
1 tablespoon tamari
2 tablespoons water
a good dash of Tabasco sauce
1 tablespoon balsamic vinegar

To serve:
pesto (see page 12)
Greek or sheep's milk yoghurt

Mix all the marinade ingredients together in a large bowl. Peel the potatoes and score them all over with a sharp knife. Cut into slices no more than 1cm thick, then place in the bowl with the marinade and leave for at least 10 minutes. Place over the grill on a medium heat for 15–17 minutes, turning regularly to prevent burning. As the potato slices start to soften, you can brush them with some of the remaining marinade.

Baste the asparagus with more of the marinade and place on the grill, medium heat again, for 2–3 minutes on each side, watching that they don't fall through the gaps. If you prefer, you can push a couple of skewers through 5 or 6 spears at a time, which will make them easier to handle and stop them falling through.

Finally, place the tomatoes on the hot plate of the barbecue, if you have one (otherwise just put them straight on the grill). This will allow you to bash them about a bit with a wooden spoon so they burst, release their juices and turn almost to a sauce.

You can plate this if you like before serving, a few potato slices per person, topped with the asparagus and the bashed tomato. A spoonful of pesto on top and a dollop of yoghurt looks as good as it tastes.

Corn on the Cob Grilled and Served Half a Dozen Ways

Here are several ideas, for all of which you have to prepare and cook the corn as follows. First, soak the cobs, still in their husks, in cold salted water for 30 minutes. Peel back the husks and remove the hairy bit, then pull the husks back over the cobs to protect them from the high heat. Place them on a hot barbecue for 15 minutes, turning them once. Then remove the husks, dip the cobs into the salted water again and return them to a medium heat for another 8–10 minutes, again turning them over to make sure that they are charred all the way round.

ALL THE SUGGESTIONS BELOW SERVE 4

With Butter and Harissa:
40g softened butter
1 tablespoon harissa (see page 13)

Put the softened butter and harissa in a bowl large enough to hold the grilled cobs and beat until combined. Add the cobs to the bowl, toss to coat them in the butter and eat at once.

With Butter, Lime and Garlic:
40g softened butter
juice of 1 lime
1 garlic clove, finely chopped
sea salt and freshly ground black pepper

Put all the ingredients in a large bowl and beat until combined. Toss with the grilled cobs and serve at once.

With Coconut Milk, Tamari and
   Thai Curry Paste:
150ml coconut milk
1 tablespoon tamari
juice of ½ lime
1 teaspoon red or green Thai curry paste
a small bunch of coriander,
   roughly chopped

Mix all the ingredients except the coriander together. When the cobs are ready, baste them generously with the sauce. Return to the grill for a couple of minutes, then remove and toss with the remaining sauce and the coriander.

With Butter and Garam Masala:
40g softened butter
1 teaspoon good-quality garam masala
or curry powder
¼ red onion or 1 shallot (golden shallot),
   very finely chopped

Mix all the ingredients together and either spread on the hot corn or place in a large bowl and toss with the cobs.

With Sweet Chilli Sauce and Lemon
   myrtle-infused Macadamia Oil:
4 teaspoons good-quality sweet chilli
   sauce
3–4 tablespoons lemon myrtle-infused
   macadamia oil

Mix the chilli sauce and oil together and baste the grilled corn with half the mixture. Return to the grill for a couple of minutes, then baste with the remainder and serve.

With Olive Oil and Dukka:
3–4 tablespoons olive oil
4 teaspoons dukka (see page 13)

Mix, baste hot corn, eat.

Aubergines with Haloumi and Fried Tortillas

Both the barbecue and the naked flame of a gas stove impart a wonderful smokiness to the aubergine (eggplant). I can't count the number of times I've made this as a last-minute standby. People always like it and resolve to try it themselves. It looks good, especially served with all the trimmings as below.

Now, if you want to make a traditional baba ghanoush (as opposed to my version on page 66), this is the place to start. You just mash the peeled barbecued aubergine (eggplant) with 1 tablespoon of olive oil, 2 tablespoons of pale tahini, the juice of 1 lemon or to taste, a couple of very finely chopped garlic cloves and some sea salt. I also add a good dash of Tabasco sauce. Garnish with finely chopped parsley and serve with warm pita bread. Sometimes, if the aubergine (eggplant) seems particularly watery, I place it in a colander and break it up with a potato masher to let the excess juices run out.

SERVES 4
90ml olive oil
juice of 1 lemon (or to taste)
2 large garlic cloves, very finely
    chopped
a good dash of Tabasco sauce
4 long, slender, firm and unblemished
    aubergines (eggplants) – fatter
    ones will work too; they just
    take longer to cook
a packet of flour tortillas
sea salt
fresh basil and/or coriander leaves,
    to garnish

For the griddled haloumi:
1 packet of haloumi cheese,
    cut into 8–10 slices
olive oil for brushing
a dash of Tabasco sauce

Make a dressing by mixing together 4 tablespoons of the olive oil, the lemon juice, garlic, Tabasco and some salt. Set aside.

Place the aubergines (eggplants) on the barbecue and cook, turning regularly, for 7–8 minutes, until they are charred all over and the skin comes away easily. Prick with a fork to test that the flesh is completely soft right through. Transfer the aubergines (eggplants) to a board and make cuts in each one about 1cm apart, without cutting all the way through. Either remove the charred skin by inserting the point of a fine blade under it and lifting it off or serve as is, so people can remove the skin themselves. Place the aubergines (eggplants) on a serving plate and douse generously with the dressing, then garnish with the herbs.

For the haloumi, brush the cheese slices lightly with olive oil and Tabasco, place on the barbecue and cook until attractively striated on both sides and just molten. Meanwhile, heat the remaining olive oil in a frying pan and fry the tortillas, one at a time, until golden on both sides, puffy and patched with black.

Serve the aubergines (eggplants) and haloumi with Chickpea and Broad Bean Salad (see page 157). Tear the fried tortillas into pieces, with which to collect the chickpeas, the soft flesh of the aubergine (eggplant), and the spicy dressing.

Pumpkin with Baby Courgettes, Red Onion, Tomato and Chermoula

Now here's a simple idea which depends entirely for its results on how well and how thoroughly you cook the vegetables. Once again, it's important that you go for the burn – there must be nothing anaemic about these vegetables, nothing half-baked and, most crucially, nothing hard. The baby courgettes (zucchini) should shrivel under the heat, their inner flesh rendered sweet and juicy. The pumpkin, when very well browned, will form a mottled skin over an orange, caramelised mush. The tomato will positively explode and turn to a slushy, intensely flavoured mess that you will want to mop up with bread. The red onion should be softly pink, and fringed with black. Adding the pungency of the chermoula, which with its cumin, paprika, coriander and lemon is as Middle Eastern as it comes, turns these basic, everyday vegetables into a plate of kaleidoscopic taste.

And of course chermoula is only one possibility. Extra harissa by the side, a lovely bright green pesto (see page 12), curry paste stirred into a little coconut milk, the sweet and sour dressing you will find in the Asian-inspired salad on page 91, even a balsamic dressing made with balsamic vinegar, extra virgin olive oil and finely chopped garlic, will all turn this plateful of vegetables, so uncomplicated in its preparation, into a feast.

Cut a quarter of a smallish Crown Prince or Jap pumpkin into quarter-moon slices no more than 1cm thick. You don't need to peel them. Score the flesh and marinate as for the sweet potatoes on page 46, setting them aside for an hour or so. Grill over a low to medium heat for 7–8 minutes on each side. Meanwhile, cut a large red onion into quarters, baste with olive oil and grill for 15 minutes, turning regularly.

The courgettes (zucchini) can be left whole if very small or cut in half. Baste them with olive oil and lemon juice and grill for 6–7 minutes, turning them so they are evenly charred. Place in a bowl and douse with more lemon juice, olive oil and a little finely chopped garlic.

A couple of thick slices of pumpkin, 2 or 3 courgette (zucchini) halves, dripping with juice, a chunk of grilled onion, half a blackened and bashed tomato, cooked as on page 46, and a little chermoula (see page 12) on top works well.

Garlic-dripping, Alcohol-drenched Field Mushrooms

Serve this with garlic bread that has been toasted on the barbecue (see page 44). Alternatively, you could have a stack of small ciabatta or Turkish bread rolls grilled and ready to receive the mushrooms. Mayonnaise, to which you've added either finely chopped garlic or the soft garlic paste below, plus lime juice and chopped chilli, or peeled, chopped, chargrilled chilli, would only add to the succulence of the experience.

SERVES 4
2 tablespoons olive oil
2 tablespoons tamari
2 tablespoons water
3 tablespoons red wine, marsala,
    brandy or a mixture of these
2 garlic cloves, finely chopped
4 field mushrooms
a small bunch of parsley or basil,
    roughly chopped

Mix together the oil, tamari, water, wine and garlic and marinate the mushrooms in this mixture for at least 10 minutes. Then place on the hot grill for 5–6 minutes on each side, until soft and cooked right through – no raw bits, please. This is an occasion when bashing the mushrooms is useful, to release their juices. Scatter the chopped parsley or basil on top and serve with any remaining marinade poured over. Expect an inky, dribbling mess.

Barbecued Whole Heads of Garlic

Just leave whole heads of garlic, either plain or lightly basted with olive oil and a little sea salt, on the narrow shelf above the grill, if your barbecue has one (alternatively, you can wrap the garlic in foil and cook in a moderate oven for 20–25 minutes). The garlic will be as soft as butter. Slice the bottoms off and squeeze out the intense paste on to bruschetta or chargrilled vegetables.

Potatoes with Garlic and Herb Yoghurt

If there are children around, you can't make too many of these. They'll be devoured in no time. You can also jam several of the cooked potatoes on to a skewer and return them to the grill for a minute before serving them with the yoghurt. By the way, if your barbecue doesn't have a shelf, parboil the potatoes first, then proceed as below.

SERVES 4
125g Greek yoghurt
1 garlic clove, finely chopped
a small bunch of chives and parsley,
    finely chopped
500g small, waxy salad potatoes,
    scrubbed
2 tablespoons olive oil
sea salt and freshly ground
    black pepper

Mix the yoghurt with the garlic and herbs, season with salt and pepper and set aside.

Place the potatoes in a bowl and mix with the olive oil and some salt and pepper, then place them on the shelf above the barbecue and cook over a low to medium heat for 15–17 minutes, until tender. You can now throw them on to the hot plate with any remaining seasoned oil and break them up a bit with tongs for a minute or two, turning them over to stop them burning. Serve at once, with the garlic and herb yoghurt.

If your barbecue doesn't have a shelf, parboil the potatoes first and place on the hot plate for 10 minutes, moving them around regularly and adding the seasoned oil. Serve as above.

Mango Cheeks with Sweet Chilli Sauce

Mango (and the pineapple option given below) crosses the sweet/savoury divide exceptionally well.

Allow 1 mango cheek (in other words, a thick slice taken off one side of the stone) per person. Score it in diagonal criss-crosses, without cutting all the way through, so when the time comes, you can open it out to reveal diamond-shaped lozenges. Place skin-side down on the barbecue grill for 7–8 minutes, then turn it on to the flesh side for 2 minutes. Brush each one with about a teaspoon of sweet chilli sauce and serve. They're great with marinated tofu steaks (see page 45) or as a sweet ending with coconut milk and a little palm sugar.

You can do something similar with a ripe pineapple, cut into 8 segments. Sprinkle with a little brown sugar and leave for up to an hour, to sweeten and soften the pineapple. Put on the grill and cook for 5–6 minutes. Then mix half a can of coconut milk with the juice of ½ lime, 2 tablespoons of rum, a small piece of chilli, finely chopped, and a handful of chopped coriander and pour over the pineapple before eating. You may want to omit the chilli and coriander if serving this as a sweet, but don't feel that you have to.

Laidback Lunch

Having come up with these nifty little chapter titles, I was brought down to earth by a screaming question. In whose life? In whose dream? In my dreams and probably in yours is the answer. I even have a fantasy of people at work taking it in turns to put together simple, delicious meals. It beats huddling around the microwave with a glossily packaged, mediocre apology for a meal, doesn't it? In the meantime, our busy lives dictate that lunchtime eating is reserved for weekends and holidays, which usually means friends, family, children – I find excuses to invite people round. Sometimes everyone contributes something to the table, the Australian way. At other times I insist on doing it all myself, not as a chore, far from it, but as an all-absorbing expression of everything that is in me to give. I rarely feel more in tune with myself and with life than when I am cooking for people I care about. It all just flows, without thought. And it seems to be so for an increasing number of people. We've become very much more relaxed about the whole business of cooking, eating, entertaining – we love our open-plan kitchens, and our shelves of cookery books and favourite cookery shows help to make us all more adventurous. The trick is to keep it as informal as possible (I've been known to greet my guests still wrapped in a towel!). I rarely set a table for lunch these days, preferring to lay everything out so that people can help themselves, sit where they like and talk to whom they like. The laughter, and the rapport, comes by itself. That, to me, is part of the enjoyment of love and life.

A Moorish and Middle Eastern Mezze Platter

I love the sight of a table laden with gorgeous-looking food. Apart from the fact that abundance in food is deeply imbedded in my psyche, I adore the sheer artistry of it – the colours, the smells, the sense of plenty. Some people fear losing control when faced with so much choice, like a kid in a sweet shop. So when I say that I love the abundance of it all, I also recommend that you treat it with a certain respect, a certain elegance, a certain watchfulness . . .

You're probably already familiar with most of the dishes below but I am including the recipes because I never want to be presented with a plastic tub of anything ever again. The combination works well – the colours vivid, the flavours bright and sprightly. There's no reason why you couldn't add the Kaitaifi Pastries on page 141 if you want to make a feast (or even an evening meal) of this, rather than a lunchtime platter. A basket of bread – warm pita or toasted Turkish or ciabatta – is essential, as is a green salad or, if time allows, the Lebanese Fattoush on page 90.

Houmous

Most people know the trick of using a whole can of chickpeas to make a bowl of houmous. Sometimes I don't even bother taking them out of the tin, simply draining off most of the liquid, seasoning appropriately, adding olive oil and introducing my stick blender into the tin for a minute of careful, then faster blitzing, but I don't necessarily recommend such laziness. The recipe here is hardly any more bother but it's more interesting because of the tahini – and more authentic, for that matter.

SERVES 4–6
1 can of chickpeas, all but 1 tablespoon of the liquid discarded
1 tablespoon pale tahini (optional)
1 garlic clove, very finely chopped
½ teaspoon ground cumin
1½ teaspoons lemon juice
5 tablespoons olive oil, plus extra to serve
a little paprika (optional)
sea salt and freshly ground black pepper

Put the chickpeas and the tablespoon of their liquid into a food processor with all the ingredients except the olive oil and paprika. Process till very smooth, drizzling in the olive oil as you do so.

Adjust the seasoning and transfer to a plate. Make a hole in the middle and pour in a little extra oil. A little paprika sprinkled on top is traditional.

Spinach with Sesame and Sumac

Sumac is the sharp, lemony, sour berry from the sumac tree. Native to the Lebanon, it is dried until dark and shrivelled, then pounded to a tart, maroon powder. Sprinkle it on to rice or couscous, yoghurt or spinach, or on to houmous, felafel and salad stuffed into a warm pita pocket. See also Lebanese Fattoush (page 90). A new must-have in the kitchen.

There's no escaping the fact that you'll need at least 2 bags of washed baby spinach if you want to make this any more than a blob on the side. Wilt the spinach in a pan, one bag at a time, with at most a spoonful of water added, stirring so the spinach doesn't stick and burn on the bottom. Squeeze out most of the excess liquid and let the spinach cool down a little, then season it with salt and pepper, a tablespoon of Greek yoghurt and 2 very finely chopped cloves of garlic. Spoon on to a couple of little mezze plates and sprinkle with a tablespoon of toasted sesame seeds and a good fat pinch of sumac.

Beetroot Tarator

I don't see half the grimace and prejudice I used to with beetroot. People have woken up to a life beyond too much cheap vinegar, so the influence of Morocco, with its cumin-macerated beetroot salads, is hugely welcome.

Preheat the oven to 200°C/Gas Mark 6. Peel 2 large beetroot and cut them into 6 pieces each, then place on a baking tray and toss them in a tablespoon of olive oil and a little salt. Cover with foil and bake for about 25 minutes, until tender. Blend in a food processor with a couple of peeled garlic cloves, the juice of ½ small lemon (or to taste), some sea salt and freshly ground black pepper and a dash of Tabasco, adding enough cold water for the blade to spin easily and reduce the beetroot to a pulp. When the beetroot is quite cold, add about 4 tablespoons of Greek yoghurt and whiz in the processor again. Serve with a fistful of fresh parsley, chopped almost to a dust, stirred through the tarator and sprinkled over it to garnish. Extra olive oil can also be swirled in at the end.

Pistachio Skordalia

This is the only version of skordalia I enjoy. The pistachios are gentler than the traditional almonds or walnuts (I've gone a bit pistachio mad in this book) and I prefer the bread soaked in water to milk. The skordalia is good served on fried or grilled aubergines (eggplants) or, like here, as one of many dips (how I loathe that word, but I am constrained).

SERVES 6
3 thick slices of stale white bread, crusts removed (about 75g once you've removed the crusts)
250ml water
3 garlic cloves, finely chopped
½ teaspoon sea salt
a pinch of white pepper
a dash of Tabasco sauce
juice of ½ lemon
4 tablespoons extra virgin olive oil
50g very fresh pistachio nuts, preferably unsalted, or adjust the salt level accordingly

Soak the bread in the water for about 10 minutes, then drain off any excess. Crush the garlic and salt in a mortar and pestle to make a soft paste, then continue in a food processor, adding the soaked bread, pepper, Tabasco and lemon juice. Whiz together for a few seconds, then add the olive oil in a thin stream. Finally add the pistachios and process for a few seconds. The sauce keeps in the fridge for at least a week and you can adjust the consistency with a little water or lemon juice if necessary.

Serve with a pile of fried flour tortillas (see page 50) or warm pita bread.

Nadine's Baba Ghanoush

This baba ghanoush is very much my interpretation but I stand by it, hand on heart. In fact, you could look on it as a cross between baba ghanoush and imam bayildi. Traditional baba ghanoush, as you'll see on page 50, is made with a peeled roasted or grilled aubergine (eggplant), is mixed with tahini and doesn't have tomatoes in it. But try this version – it's rich and gorgeous and much prettier.

SERVES 20 AS PART OF A MINI MEZZE PLATTER OR 6 AS PART OF A LUNCHTIME MEZZE PLATTER
1 large aubergine (eggplant), cut into 4cm chunks
4 tablespoons olive oil
a good pinch of sea salt
a few dashes of Tabasco sauce
1 large, ripe tomato, chopped
1 fat garlic clove, finely chopped

Preheat the oven to 180°C/Gas Mark 4. Toss the aubergine (eggplant) chunks in 3 tablespoons of the olive oil with the sea salt and Tabasco, then spread them out on a baking tray and bake for about 15 minutes, until charred and tender.

Heat the remaining oil in a frying pan, add the tomato and garlic and fry for about 30 seconds. Add the roasted aubergine (eggplant) and a couple of spoonfuls of water to loosen the mixture, then cook for about 3 minutes over a medium to high heat, till the whole lot breaks up into a rich, fleshy, black-skin-speckled 'salad'. Eat warm or cold, spooned on to warm pita or Turkish bread toasts. A dollop of thick sheep's milk yoghurt is always good to have with this.

Orange and Black Olive Salad with Red Onion, Cumin and Paprika

This traditional Moroccan salad is for Alice, who wrote to me asking for the recipe after tasting something like it in Paris.

My mother used to serve this, bar the oranges, with pre-dinner drinks. I serve it as part of a Middle Eastern-inspired mezze platter. Try it also with ruby-red grapefruit or blood oranges.

SERVES 6

3 large oranges, peel, pith and
   pips removed, thinly sliced into
   quarter moons
225g Moroccan or Provençal
   black olives
1 smallish red onion, sliced paper thin
rocket leaves, to serve

For the dressing:
2 garlic cloves, very finely chopped
1 teaspoon ground cumin
1 teaspoon sweet paprika
a small piece of red chilli, deseeded
   and finely chopped (optional)
a small handful of mint or coriander
   leaves or both, roughly torn
3 tablespoons extra virgin olive oil,
   or the more traditional argan oil
   if you can find it
a dash of Tabasco sauce
a pinch of sea salt

Mix all the ingredients for the dressing together. Put the orange slices, olives and red onion in a bowl and pour over the dressing. Mix carefully and either serve immediately or allow to macerate for an hour or so first. Scatter the rocket on top before serving.

Spinach and Ricotta Fritters with Seared Mango and Watercress Salad

These are a take on the Italian *baci*, sweet though those are. I wrote the recipe for *delicious* magazine a couple of years ago and have made them countless times since. They're so easy and you can customise them to quite some degree. I sometimes substitute 2 tablespoons of pesto for the spinach, playing on their Italian roots, with more pesto to serve.

Put aside qualms about the cultural mix and enjoy these subtle fritters and their Asian-inspired accompaniments. If possible, buy the ricotta from a good deli and ensure that it is very fresh.

SERVES 6
150g spinach
325g ricotta cheese
4 large eggs
225g Italian 'oo' flour, sifted
2 teaspoons baking powder
grated zest of 1 lemon
1 tablespoon harissa (see page 13)
    or very finely chopped red chilli
1 teaspoon lemon juice
1 litre sunflower oil for deep-frying
sea salt

For the dressing:
3 garlic cloves, very finely chopped
1 long red chilli, deseeded and
    chopped to a confetti
30g palm sugar, grated
a knob of fresh ginger, grated,
    then squeezed to extract the juice,
    flesh discarded
juice of 2 limes
1½ tablespoons tamari
2 tablespoons water
a handful of coriander leaves

**For the seared mango and
    watercress salad:**
3 perfectly ripe but still firm mangoes
2 tablespoons sunflower oil
1 tablespoon palm sugar
a small piece of red chilli,
    very finely chopped
6 handfuls of watercress

To make the dressing, simply mix all the ingredients together and set aside. Then cut the 'cheeks' (a thick slice from either side of the stone) from the mangoes, peel and slice them neatly. Heat the sunflower oil in a frying pan over a medium heat, add the palm sugar and stir until dissolved. Then add the mango slices and fry until golden brown and crisply caramelised in places. Stir in the chilli, remove from the heat and set aside while you make the fritters.

For the fritters, put the spinach in a pan, cover and place over a medium heat until wilted. Drain off any liquid and set aside to cool for a while. Combine the spinach with the ricotta, eggs, flour, baking powder, lemon zest, harissa or chilli and lemon juice and mix well.

Pour the sunflower oil into a small, deep saucepan and place over a medium heat. To test the temperature, drop a small amount of the fritter mixture into it – it should sizzle and rise to the surface. Use 2 dessertspoons to shape the fritter mixture into quenelles – neat ovals made by scraping the mixture from one spoon to another. Drop them into the hot oil, a few at a time, and cook for about 2 minutes, turning them over half way through to make sure they are golden brown all over. Transfer to a plate lined with kitchen paper to drain, then to a large flat plate.

Quickly toss the watercress in a tablespoon of the dressing and immediately pour the rest of the dressing over the fritters. Position the seared mango on top, then loosely pile the watercress on top of that. Serve without delay, to take advantage of the fluffiness of the fritters and the pertness of the watercress.

Corn and Courgette Fritters with Avocado and Tomato, Chilli and Cumin Jam

This is in the lunch chapter but it could just as easily be served for breakfast. Indeed, I made a Sunday ritual of corn fritters for nearly a year in one of Byron's landmark cafés.

The recipe makes much more jam than you will need here, but if you put it in sterilised jars and seal tightly it will keep for up to a year in the fridge. The courgettes (zucchini) can be green, of course.

SERVES 4–6
3 yellow courgettes (zucchini), grated
kernels from 1 superfresh corn
    on the cob
1 small red onion, very finely chopped
2 tablespoons grated haloumi,
    Gruyère or Jarlsberg cheese
    (optional) – but not Cheddar, please
2 garlic cloves, finely chopped
200g Danish feta cheese
2 large eggs, lightly beaten
1½ tablespoons dukka (see page 13)
a good handful of parsley, finely
    chopped
a good handful of coriander,
    finely chopped
120g Italian 'oo' flour, sifted
½ teaspoon baking powder
light olive oil for frying
sea salt and freshly ground
    black pepper

For the tomato, chilli and cumin jam:
1kg tomatoes, roughly chopped
1 very large red onion (about 250g),
    or 2 smaller ones, chopped
4 large garlic cloves, cut in half
200g caster sugar
200ml red wine
2 large red chillies, deseeded and
    chopped to a confetti
1½ tablespoons cumin seeds
a fat pinch of sea salt
a generous sprig of coriander
    (optional)

To serve:
2 large or 3 small perfectly ripe
    avocados
juice of 1 lime
2 tablespoons olive or macadamia oil
3–4 handfuls of rocket

For the tomato, chilli and cumin jam, put all the ingredients except the coriander into a large, heavy-based saucepan and bring to the boil. Then reduce the heat to medium and simmer for 50–60 minutes, stirring occasionally, until reduced to a jammy consistency. If you're using the coriander, add the sprig at the end for a couple of minutes to wilt.

Rinse out a couple of small jars with boiling water and dry in a low oven. Put the hot jam in them, cover with baking parchment, cut to fit, and leave to cool completely, then seal.

Grate the courgettes (zucchini) into a large bowl and add the corn kernels, red onion, grated cheese and garlic. Crumble in the feta and mix well with your hand. Then mix in the eggs, dukka and chopped herbs, followed by the flour and baking powder. Season with pepper – you probably won't need salt because of the feta.

Before you cook the fritters, peel and stone the avocados and slice them into half moons. Squeeze the lime juice over them, drizzle with the oil and season with salt and pepper. Toss with the rocket and set aside.

To cook the fritters, heat about 5mm oil in a large frying pan and line a plate with several layers of kitchen paper. Drop generous spoonfuls of the mixture into the hot oil, about 3 or 4 at a time (leave plenty of space between them, as they will spread), and fry for 50–60 seconds, until browned underneath. Turn to brown the other side, then transfer to the paper-lined plate to drain.

Serve 3 or 4 per person, a mound of avocado and rocket over them or by the side, depending on your aesthetic, and an ample spoonful of the jam.

Artichokes with Sun-dried Tomatoes and Preserved Lemon Dressing

A recipe from *The Cranks Bible* (Weidenfeld & Nicolson, 2001). I often make it and don't tire of it, so I don't feel bad about including it here too, with a few adjustments here and there because one lives and learns. Serve with warm rustic bread and a salad of wild rocket tossed with a little oil, balsamic vinegar, crushed sea salt and freshly ground black pepper and shavings of the best Parmesan.

SERVES 4

6 fresh artichokes (or use artichokes preserved in oil, thickly sliced)
½ lemon
2 tablespoons olive oil
saffron stock made by infusing a pinch of good-quality saffron in 200ml hot water
1 garlic clove, very finely sliced
20 black olives, preferably herbed Provençal ones
12 sun-dried tomatoes in oil
2 tablespoons pine nuts, lightly toasted in a dry frying pan
1 tablespoon finely chopped parsley

For the dressing:
1 small preserved lemon
6 tablespoons extra virgin olive oil
1 garlic clove, finely sliced
1 tablespoon hot water
a dash of Tabasco sauce

Make the dressing by whizzing all the ingredients together in a blender, then set aside.

If you are using fresh artichokes, slice off the top third of each one, then cook them in plenty of salted water, adding the lemon half to the pan to stop them turning black. After about 45 minutes, when the artichokes are tender (i.e. when a leaf can be pulled off easily), remove from the pan and pull off the leaves. Scoop out the hairy choke with a teaspoon and cut each artichoke into thick slices.

Heat the olive oil in a large frying pan, add the artichoke slices and fry over a fairly high heat for 6–8 minutes, until golden brown all over. Half way through, begin to add the saffron stock and the sliced garlic, stirring all the time, until most of the liquid has evaporated or been absorbed to create a thick, pungent coating sauce. Add the olives and sun-dried tomatoes to the pan, then add the preserved lemon dressing, plus a little hot water if necessary to loosen it. Remove from the heat and garnish generously with the toasted pine nuts and chopped parsley. Allow to cool a little before serving.

Salt and Pepper Tofu Caesar

I found this in a Byron Bay café called Fresh, which is almost an institution. For many years it seemed quintessentially Byron Bay to me: the food bright, simple, abundant and good; part focal point for locals, part tourist trap, poised as it is mere metres from the beach. Like the rest of Byron, it has gone through various incarnations, and now all that remains is the tourist trap bit. Even this favourite salad has gone but I include it here – my version of it at least – in acknowledgement of the integrity and simple pleasures that once made this place so special.

You only need the inner leaves of the lettuces. The outer leaves can be roughly chopped and braised with petits pois, the French way, with a little softened onion and garlic and a pinch of sugar.

SERVES 4–6

3 Cos or romaine lettuces, inner, tender pale leaves only
18 slices from a baguette or Turkish loaf
2 large garlic cloves, cut in half
75ml olive oil
1 quantity of Salt and Pepper Tofu (see page 130)

For the dressing:
2 large eggs
juice of 1 lemon
a few splashes of Worcestershire sauce or Bragg Liquid Amino (a rather good product behind all that scientific terminology, available from healthfood shops)
100ml olive oil
30g Parmesan cheese, freshly grated
sea salt and freshly ground black pepper

Preheat the oven to 180°C/Gas Mark 4. Wash the lettuce leaves, putting them in a salad spinner to dry, if you have one, or loosely bundling them into a dry tea towel and swinging them around a few times. Set aside.

To make the croûtons, rub the bread slices with the cut garlic cloves until the bread is softened by the juices. Toss in the olive oil, then spread out on a baking tray and bake for about 20 minutes, until crisp and golden.

Meanwhile, prepare the dressing. Boil the eggs for exactly 1 minute, then drain. Break them into a large bowl and whisk in the lemon juice, the Worcestershire sauce or Bragg Liquid Amino, olive oil and a good pinch of sea salt and black pepper. Stir in the grated cheese.

Put the lettuce, croûtons and tofu in a large bowl, add the dressing and mix together, light as air. Serve in large bowls while the croûtons and tofu are still warm, the batter still crisp and translucent. And spare a thought for Byron Bay.

Rocket, Turkish Fig and Goat's Cheese Salad with Pomegranate Dressing

Pomegranates were an integral part of my childhood. I'm always cheered by the sight of them and love the inevitable mess. From a small, rounded shrub with narrow, leathery, dark leaves and attractive scarlet or variegated flowers, the fruit itself is typically deep pink or rich red, with tough, leathery skin. Before eating, remove the bitter, spongy membrane that separates the seeds into compartments. Serve this for lunch or as a starter to just about anything in this book, especially anything Middle Eastern. In Australia you could use the lovely Meredith goat's cheese marinated in olive oil; in the UK any goat's cheese marinated in olive oil or even feta in oil. For the dressing, ideally you should use the very brightest, freshest, reddest, sweetest pomegranate you can find. If it isn't the season for pomegranates, however, just add a little more water to the dressing and a pinch of sugar.

SERVES 6

12 pecan nuts, or to taste, broken
    into pieces
240g wide-leafed rocket
9 large, fleshy, semi-dried Turkish
    figs, cut into thick slivers
240g goat's cheese marinated
    in olive oil
½ small red onion, sliced paper thin

For the pomegranate dressing:

4 tablespoons extra virgin olive oil
1½ teaspoons pomegranate molasses
1 tablespoon water
a dash of Tabasco sauce (optional)
1 pomegranate, with firm, red,
    glossy skin
sea salt and freshly ground
    black pepper

For the dressing, mix together the olive oil, pomegranate molasses, water, Tabasco, if using, and some salt and pepper. Cut the pomegranate into quarters and hold a quarter back. Squeeze the juice from the rest into the dressing.

Toast the pecans for 8 minutes in a dry frying pan. Put the rocket, figs, goat's cheese, red onion and pecans into a bowl and toss with the dressing. Dismantle the remaining pomegranate into separate seeds and scatter them like jewels over the salad.

Roasted Beetroot and Fennel with Dukka, Griddled Haloumi and Croûtons

I first made this addictive salad using Gympie goat's cheese (an Australian cheese similar to the English Golden Cross). I still believe it goes well with beetroot but I finally opted for haloumi, since it is closer to the Middle Eastern derivation of this dish. Finding a French-style chèvre isn't easy where I live, so imagine how pleased I was to discover Gympie cheese, made by a Frenchman, Camille Mortaud, in the Queensland town of Gympie. If serving this recipe with Golden Cross or mature Gympie goat's cheese, slice a 240g goat's cheese log into 12, using a hot knife to give you good, clean slices. Just before serving, dip each slice into water, then dust with flour. Heat a little olive oil in a frying pan and fry the cheese until golden on both sides. Drain on kitchen paper and serve straight away.

SERVES 6

a large bunch of baby beetroot
120ml olive oil, plus extra for brushing
Tabasco sauce, to taste
2 smallish fennel bulbs,
    cut into 8 pieces each
2 tablespoons extra virgin olive oil
2 teaspoons balsamic vinegar
6 tablespoons dukka (see page 13)
a small handful of parsley, finely
    chopped (optional)
1 packet of haloumi cheese
1 quantity of Turkish Croûtons
    (see page 90)
1 small red onion, very thinly
    sliced into half moons
4 handfuls of rocket
1 lemon, cut into 6 wedges
sea salt and freshly ground
    black pepper

Preheat the oven to 180°C/Gas Mark 4. Wash the beetroot and trim off all but 1cm of each stalk. Cut them into halves or quarters, depending on size, then place on a large baking tray. Pour over half the olive oil and season with salt, pepper and Tabasco. Roast for about 25 minutes, until tender, checking them regularly and turning as necessary to prevent burning. You can cover the beetroot with foil if it looks as if it is charring too soon. When it is ready, the skin will look a little shrivelled and the beetroot will be tender and sweet.

Put the fennel on a baking tray, season with salt and pepper and pour over the remaining olive oil. Roast for about 20 minutes, until it, too, is tender and lightly browned. Transfer both beetroot and fennel to a serving plate with the hot oil and drizzle over the extra virgin olive oil and balsamic vinegar. Then add the dukka and the parsley, if using, and mix carefully.

For the haloumi, cut the cheese into slices about 1mm thick, then into small strips, as thick as a chip but half as long. Brush them lightly with olive oil. Place on a hot ridged griddle and cook until attractively charred and just molten.

Mix the beetroot and fennel with the hot haloumi, the croûtons, the finely sliced onion and, at the last possible moment, the rocket. Serve at once, with wedges of lemon by the side.

Yellow Beetroot
At this year's Noosa Food Festival I picked up some golf-ball sized golden beetroot. The next day, wrapped in newspaper, they made the trip back to Byron (all 300km of it). I boiled them for 45 minutes, let them cool, peeled them and sliced them thinly into half moons. Then I doused them with 1½ tablespoons of macadamia oil, a teaspoon of Chardonnay vinegar, a little Murray River salt (for which read Maldon salt in the UK), ½ teaspoon of coarsly pestled green peppercorns and a talespoon of powder-fine chopped parsley and ran my fingers through the lot over and over again, massaging the seasonings into the softly receptive golden beets. Such a simple treat.

Pistachio-battered Haloumi and Aubergine Galettes with Tomato and Olive Salsa, Sesame-roasted Sweet Potato Chips and Basil Mayonnaise

These galettes are simply slices of fried aubergine (eggplant). The pistachio-battered haloumi fritters have many useful applications. Try them with Tomato, Chilli and Cumin Jam (page 70) or Fig, Pecan and Port Jam (page 124), Spinach with Sesame and Sumac (page 63), any of the yoghurt sauces in this book, as a side to Lebanese Fattoush (page 90), with blanched cauliflower florets mixed with the same sumac-flavoured red onion and dressing as the fattoush, or simply with chermoula (page 12) or harissa (page 13).

SERVES 4

120g pistachio nuts, lightly toasted in a dry frying pan, then sliced
1 small packet (120g) tempura batter, made up according to the manufacturer's instructions
1 plump garlic clove, finely chopped
3 tablespoons finely chopped parsley
1 teaspoon finely ground lemon myrtle (optional)
a fat pinch of sea salt
1 teaspoon ground green or black peppercorns
1 packet of haloumi cheese, broken into rough pieces about 4cm across
sunflower oil for deep-frying
1 quantity of Sesame-roasted Sweet Potato Chips (see page 158)

For the aubergine (eggplant):
2 long, thin aubergines (eggplants), thinly sliced
light olive oil for frying
juice of ½ lemon
a dash of Tabasco sauce
sea salt

To serve:
Tomato and Olive Salsa (see page 14)
4 generous tablespoons mayonnaise, mixed with a generous handful of finely shredded basil (or, if you can do it, mayonnaise made with basil-infused olive oil)

Prepare the aubergine (eggplant) slices by frying them in about 1cm of very hot oil till golden on both sides. Drain on layers of kitchen paper, season with the lemon juice and Tabasco and some salt and keep warm (in the oven, covered in foil, works well).

To make the haloumi fritters, mix the sliced pistachios into the tempura batter with the garlic, herbs, salt and pepper. Dip the haloumi pieces into the batter. Heat the sunflower oil in a small, deep pan and fry the battered haloumi a few pieces at a time until they rise to the surface and are evenly gold all over. Transfer to a plate triple lined with kitchen paper and leave to drain.

To serve, arrange several slices of aubergine (eggplant) on each plate in a small, concentric circle, top with a mound of the sweet potato chips, then a spoonful of salsa, then the haloumi fritters and finally a tablespoon of the basil mayonnaise.

Salad of Baby Spinach, Feta Cheese, Medjool Dates, Red Onion and Pecans with Ras-al-hanout Spiced Dressing

A friend for whom I had prepared this salad for lunch declared it to be 'food made in heaven'. Try it, because nothing can quite prepare you for the utter surprise of the rosebuds in the ras-al-hanout. I don't know about heaven, but there is something rather otherworldly and intoxicating about it.

SERVES 4

1 tablespoon butter
1 large, ripe but firm pear,
    cored and sliced
a dash of Tabasco sauce
8 pecan nuts, broken into quarters
150g baby spinach
120g soft, mild feta cheese,
    cut into strips
8 Medjool dates, pitted and sliced
    into eighths
½ small red onion, very finely
    sliced into half moons

For the dressing:
1 quantity of ras-al-hanout
    (see page 14)
a handful of fresh coriander, tough
    stalks removed
a squeeze of lemon juice
120ml extra virgin olive oil
2 tablespoons balsamic vinegar

For the dressing, put the ras-al-hanout in a mortar, add the coriander and lemon juice and pound for a few moments. Mix in the olive oil and balsamic vinegar and set aside.

Melt the butter in a frying pan, add the pear slices and fry for a few minutes, until just translucent. Season with the Tabasco and leave to cool slightly.

Toast the pecans in a dry fying pan for 8 minutes. Delicately pile all the salad ingredients, including the pear, on to a large plate and carefully mix with 6 tablespoons of the dressing (the extra dressing can be reserved for later use). Serve at once.

Thai Green Papaya Salad (Som Dtam)

It's not always easy to find green papaya in the UK (I have a papaya tree in my garden – lucky me). Try Asian shops or even your local Thai restaurant, which might be able to procure one for you with enough notice. I can't think of a better thing to eat before one of the curries in this book (see pages 134–137). Additional garnishes such as toasted crushed peanuts, fried shallots (golden shallots) – or, traditionally, dried shrimps, but don't ask me about those – can be sprinkled over the salad at the end.

With thanks to Tippi Heng, for many years one of Byron's favourite chefs, who showed me how to make this.

SERVES 4–6

1 green papaya (it should be
    completely green and very firm,
    with no yellow bits at all)
2 garlic cloves, chopped
1–2 large red chillies, deseeded
2 shallots (golden shallots), chopped
palm sugar, to taste
light soy sauce or nam pla
    (Thai fish sauce), to taste
juice of 1 large lime
8 cherry tomatoes, halved

Peel and deseed the papaya, then shred the flesh using either a mandoline or the vegetable shredding attachment of a food processor (or, if all else fails, a grater).

Using a mortar and pestle, pound the garlic, chillies and shallots (golden shallots) to a fine paste. Add the palm sugar, soy or fish sauce and lime juice, then taste and adjust the seasoning.

In a large bowl, mix the shredded papaya with the cherry tomatoes and dressing. Gently bruise all the ingredients with a pestle, then serve.

Cumin-braised Baby Carrots in Lime and Harissa Vinaigrette with Rocket, Goat's Cheese and Walnuts

This pretty well encapsulates the way I cook and eat. My mother serves cumin-braised carrots as a side dish with braises and roasts and I often do the same with these baby carrots. But something my mother would not have considered is turning them into the main focus, as I have done here. When I started writing this book, I wanted to take a singularly Australian approach to food – which at the time meant that the recipes would have a predominantly Asian slant. Then, in the time it took to get the book off the ground (don't ask), another influence came into play: cumin and harissa, dukka and ras-al-hanout, the spicing of the Middle East and North Africa making a steady onslaught on the Antipodean kitchen. And this suits me fine. If there is an Australian influence, it is in the celebration of the warm salad.

SERVES 4
50ml extra virgin olive oil
500g bunched baby carrots,
    2cm of top left on
½ teaspoon ground cumin
2 teaspoons cumin seeds
150ml good-quality vegetable stock
3 garlic cloves, finely sliced
a thumb-sized piece of long red chilli,
    finely chopped
4 large handfuls of wild rocket
a large handful of walnuts (as fresh
    as possible), lightly toasted in
    a dry frying pan
120g goat's cheese, crumbled (in
    Australia use Meredith goat's
    cheese marinated in olive oil)
sea salt and freshly ground
    black pepper

For the vinaigrette:
1 garlic clove, finely chopped
grated zest of 2 limes
2–3 tablespoons lime juice
1 spring onion (shallot), finely chopped
½ red chilli, finely chopped
½ teaspoon cumin seeds, lightly
    toasted and partly pounded
½ teaspoon coriander seeds, lightly
    toasted and pounded
¼ teaspoon strong mustard
4 tablespoons olive oil
2 tablespoons chopped parsley
1 teaspoon harissa
sea salt

Heat the olive oil in a pan large enough to hold the carrots lying flat, then add the carrots, ground cumin and cumin seeds and sauté for 4–5 minutes. Add the stock and garlic and bring to the boil. Cover the pan, reduce to a simmer and cook for about 20 minutes, checking occasionally that the carrots are not drying out – a little sticking to the bottom is desirable but adjust the heat level or add more liquid as you see fit. Remove the lid and continue to cook for 3–4 minutes to reduce most of the remaining liquid, shaking the pan about so the carrots become seductively browned and coated in a sticky, golden sauce. Season with salt and pepper and stir in the chilli.

Put all the ingredients for the dressing in a jar with a lid and shake well to amalgamate. Put the carrots, rocket, toasted walnuts and goat's cheese in a bowl and toss with the dressing. Divide between 4 plates and serve.

New Potato, Green Bean and Green Olive Salad with Chermoula and Harissa Dressing

This is a Moroccan triple whammy even if it is completely made up. You see, I just trust that by the time you've started cooking from this book you'll have all these things to hand. Expect a rich and intensely flavoured salad, copiously coated in a deep and powerful seasoned dressing.

SERVES 4

650g small, waxy salad potatoes,
   peeled and thickly sliced
200g green beans
12 green olives
4 handfuls of rocket or baby spinach

For the dressing:

5 tablespoons extra virgin olive oil
   (or argan oil, if available)
1 tablespoon lemon juice
1 small piece of preserved lemon,
   finely chopped
5 tablespoons chermoula
   (see page 12)
1 tablespoon harissa (see page 13)

Mix together all the ingredients for the dressing and set aside.

Put the potatoes in a pan of salted water, bring to the boil and simmer until tender. When they are half done, add the green beans. When the potatoes and beans are tender, drain well. While they are still piping hot (all the better to absorb the dressing), mix them with the dressing and the green olives. Cool slightly, then add to the rocket or spinach and mix carefully with 2 forks – or your fingers. Serve at once, piled on to individual plates.

Nadine's Chouchouka with Baked Eggs

Chouchouka is a very oily Tunisian salad with fried rather than grilled peppers (capsicums), which tend to include green. This, however, is my somewhat Italianised version and I can't stand green peppers, so they've been kicked out. The baked eggs on top usually go on a rich tomato sauce and they were an easy lunch or supper of my childhood. Warm bread to mop up the sauce is pretty much obligatory. I cook the tomato sauce in a frying pan because I really want it to fry and considerably reduce – it mustn't be at all watery.

SERVES 2–4

1 red and 1 yellow pepper (capsicum)
4–5 tablespoons olive oil
1 large red onion, roughly chopped
4 garlic cloves, 2 very finely chopped,
    2 left whole
400g canned chopped tomatoes
1 bay leaf
4 eggs
sea salt and freshly ground black
    pepper

Place the peppers (capsicums) over a naked flame and cook, turning them a couple of times, until they are completely charred all the way round. If that's not an option, place them under a hot grill (you'll find that peppers charred over an open flame cook faster than under the grill, so the flesh doesn't go as soft or start to weep). When they are done, either cover with a tea towel to loosen the skin or simply run them under cold water. Remove the skin, pith and seeds and cut the flesh into strips. Fry the pepper (capsicum) strips for a minute or so with just a drop of the oil, then remove from the pan and set aside.

Heat the rest of the oil in a large frying pan, add the onion and fry till soft, adding the chopped garlic half way through. Then add the tomatoes, whole garlic cloves and the bay leaf. Bring to the boil, reduce the heat a little and simmer quite briskly for at least 25 minutes, stirring regularly to prevent sticking. Season to taste.

Preheat the oven to 180°C/Gas Mark 4. Add the peppers (capsicums) to the sauce and cook for 5–6 minutes, stirring all the time. Transfer to a dish – a round, earthenware French dish is perfect – make 4 indentations in the sauce and break in the eggs. Place in the oven and bake for about 8 minutes, till the whites are well set and the yolks still have a little wobble. Serve at once.

Potatoes with White Asparagus, Griddled Peppers, Mushrooms and Poached Duck Eggs

This came about after a visit to the farmers' market on the last day of photography for this book. I shopped and Ian snapped. And I had to do something with it all, didn't I? Seeing as this is the only recipe for duck eggs in the book, I'll throw in an extra one just for luck. Blanch 200g broad beans, drain and refresh in cold water, then slip off their skins. Add them to a bowl of mixed leaves, including watercress if possible – it cuts through the richness of the eggs. Throw in a skinned, grilled red pepper (capsicum), cut into strips, and a small red onion, very finely sliced. Deseed and dice a large, ripe tomato and fry it in a film of olive oil for less than a minute. Toss with a dressing made of 2 tablespoons of Dijon mustard, 1½ tablespoons of Chardonnay vinegar, a very finely chopped clove of garlic and 4 tablespoons of extra virgin olive oil, then place 2 warm poached duck eggs on top. This makes a generous lunch for two.

SERVES 4

2 bunches (about 450g) white
    asparagus, trimmed
4 tablespoons olive oil
75g butter
600g small, waxy salad potatoes,
    peeled and cut into slices 1cm thick
2 garlic cloves, finely sliced
500g brown-cap or chestnut
    mushrooms, cut in half if large
4 tablespoons brandy
2 tablespoons tamari
1 red pepper (capsicum), roasted,
    skinned, deseeded and cut into
    thin strips
4 free-range duck eggs, poached
    for 2–3 minutes (see page 24)
a small handful of sage leaves
salt and freshly ground black pepper

Blanch the asparagus in a large pan of boiling salted water for 3–4 minutes, then drain and refresh in cold water. Set aside.

Heat the oil and 60g of the butter in a large frying pan and add the potatoes. Season them with salt, pepper and the sliced garlic and fry for 15 minutes, turning occasionally, until tender and golden brown. Transfer the potatoes to a bowl, leaving the butter and oil in the pan. Add the mushrooms to the pan, together with the brandy and tamari. Fry vigorously for 8–10 minutes. This might seem too long for mushrooms but you will release layers of taste and necessary juices. Return the potatoes to the pan and simmer for a couple of minutes to reduce the mushroom juices a little, then add the remaining butter.

Transfer to a large dish and give the pepper strips and the asparagus a quick blast in the pan to heat them through. Add them to the potatoes and mushrooms and position the eggs on top. Drizzle with any remaining pan juices and scatter with the sage leaves. Serve at once.

Fennel Sauté with Pernod, Orange and Garlic

I have occasionally had to apologise for fennel's aniseed flavour. 'It is attenuated on slow braising,' I say, or, 'Try it in a soup with cream or a milk made from blanched, blended and pressed almonds.' Or, 'Make a carpaccio of it with a firm green apple, some itsy-bitsy, teeny-weeny capers, olive oil and Chardonnay vinegar.' But here, finally, I make no apologies. Here is fennel revelling in its own flavour, shouting out its unique liquorice sweetness. I was almost tempted to throw in some aniseed seeds just to make the point, but, hey, I know when to stop.

SERVES 4
75ml olive oil
4 small, firm and unblemished
    fennel bulbs, cut into quarters,
    fronds reserved
1 orange, cut into quarter-moon slices
    (leave the skin on), pips removed
4 garlic cloves, finely sliced
2 teaspoons brown sugar
150ml Pernod
about 250ml vegetable stock
about 12 black olives
a small handful of finely chopped
    parsley (optional)
sea salt and freshly ground
    black pepper

Heat the oil in a large frying pan and sauté the fennel quarters until they start to turn golden brown all over. Add the orange slices, garlic, brown sugar and half the Pernod. Sauté for 5–6 minutes, then add just enough vegetable stock to cover. Simmer for about 10 minutes on quite a strong heat, until the liquid is reduced to a sticky sauce and the fennel and orange slices are lightly caramelised. Add the olives, the rest of the Pernod and some salt and pepper to taste. Cook for a few minutes, adjusting the liquid and the heat as seems fit, so that the fennel is tender, golden and bathed in an orange glaze, rich with the sweet aniseedy taste of Pernod and the warmth of braised garlic.

Add the reserved fennel fronds, picked off the stem, and the parsley, if using. Transfer to a plate or leave in the pan and take the whole splendid thing to the table as it is. If you want added impact and don't think it kitsch (or don't mind – I don't), set the Pernod alight before the alcohol is cooked out and flambé it. Serve with Saffron Rice (see page 155).

The Great Ozzie Veggie Stack

When I first came to Australia, I was struck by the casual references to veggie, or 'vego', food. There was no big chest-beating, hemp-wearing crusade to accompany the very ordinary, down-to-earth business of eating your greens. Everyone, not just size-eight-chasing women, eats large salads of sparkling-fresh greens, while every café boasts its version of the Veggie Stack, which essentially consists of yummy things held together by more yummy things – pesto, chermoula, home-blitzed houmous – all abundance and just-cooked freshness.

I can't live without my Sunbeam griddle these days. It makes light work of grilling all manner of vegetables and they come out just the way they should – but of course an ordinary griddle or grill will do just fine.

If you haven't yet tried the haloumi fritters on page 77, you could give them a go here instead of grilling or frying the haloumi as described below.

SERVES 4

1 aubergine (eggplant), cut into
   about 12 finger-thick slices
120ml olive oil
juice of 1 small lemon
1 tablespoon tamari
1 tablespoon balsamic vinegar
2 garlic cloves, very finely chopped
4 finger-thick slices of sweet potato
   or butternut squash, peeled
4 large flat mushrooms
1 red onion, cut into 4 thick slices
2 artichokes, leaves and hairy choke
   removed to leave only the hearts
1 fennel bulb, fronds removed, cut
   into slices 1cm thick
2 tablespoons pesto (see page 12)
125g haloumi cheese, cut into
   4 thick slices
4 handfuls of wild rocket
20 sunblush (semi-dried) tomatoes
4 generous tablespoons Houmous
   (see page 62)
sea salt

Brush the aubergine (eggplant) slices with 4 tablespoons of the olive oil and place under a hot grill or on a ridged griddle until soft and well browned on both sides. Remove from the heat and season immediately with sea salt and a good squeeze of lemon juice.

Preheat the oven to 200°C/Gas Mark 6. Combine the tamari, vinegar, garlic and 2 tablespoons of the oil in a bowl. Brush the sweet potato or butternut squash, mushrooms, red onion, artichokes and fennel with this mixture. Transfer to a baking tray and roast for about 15–20 minutes, till tender and browned (you may need to remove the onion slices and artichokes a little earlier). Toss gently with the pesto.

Meanwhile, brush the haloumi with a little of the remaining oil and grill or fry it till golden on the outside and molten within. Lightly toss the rocket in the remaining oil and lemon juice.

To serve, make 4 stacks by setting first the mushroom in the centre of each plate, then adding the sweet potato or squash, tomatoes, aubergine (eggplant), fennel, red onion and artichoke, either cementing them with the houmous or just placing a dollop of it on top. Then top with a slice of haloumi and a handful of rocket. Drizzle with the pan juices from the roasted vegetables, which can be mopped up with warm, crusty bread.

Lebanese Fattoush

This bread salad is the Middle Eastern equivalent of the Italian panzanella but with a sharp, sour dressing that makes it more interesting to me. It's essential that you use the short Lebanese cucumbers – what we refer to as baby cucumbers in the UK. They are not only a good deal sweeter but also firmer and much crisper.

I used to make this salad with torn pita bread, macerating in the dressing, but you'll see how irresistible the fried croûtons are. Like other simple, peasant dishes, everything depends on the quality of the ingredients. There's little camouflage going on here, so every ingredient positively has to hum.

SERVES 4

4 Cos lettuce leaves, cut crossways
   into strips 3cm wide
2 large, ripe but firm tomatoes,
   roughly chopped
4 radishes, thickly sliced
2 Lebanese (baby) cucumbers, cut into
   thick half moons
a good handful of parsley, roughly
   chopped
a small handful of mint leaves,
   chopped if large, left whole if not
1 red onion, finely sliced into half
   moons
1 tablespoon finely ground sumac
1 teaspoon ras-al-hanout, harissa
   or chermoula (see pages 14, 13
   and 12)

For the Turkish croûtons:
60g butter
60ml olive oil
¼ large Turkish loaf (or ciabatta),
   split in half, then cut or torn
   into 2cm chunks

For the dressing:
1 garlic clove, peeled
1 teaspoon sea salt
3 tablespoons extra virgin olive oil
1 tablespoon white wine vinegar
juice of 1 lemon

First make the croûtons. Heat the butter and olive oil in a frying pan until foaming, then fry the bread in 2 batches until golden brown all over. Remove with a slotted spoon, drain on kitchen paper and set aside.

For the salad, mix the lettuce, tomatoes, radishes, cucumbers, parsley and mint together in a bowl. In a pestle and mortar, gently pound together the sliced onion, sumac and whichever spice paste you are using, then set aside.

For the dressing, crush the garlic with the salt and whisk in the olive oil, followed by the vinegar and lemon juice. Add the dressing to the salad, together with the croûtons and bruised onion, and toss well.

Salad of Shiitake Mushrooms, Asparagus and Lychees in Sweet Chilli and Tamarind Dressing

This is a salad of which the saying, 'Out of chaos, stars are born', is a fitting epithet. I came up with it, or a version thereof, one horribly heartbroken week with a looming deadline and a head hollowed out by grief. Somehow, this came and I enjoyed it.

SERVES 2

2 bunches (about 450g) asparagus, tough ends snapped off
16 shiitake mushrooms
12 lychees, peeled and pitted
a good handful of rocket
a few mint leaves
a few small basil leaves
1 teaspoon sesame seeds, lightly toasted in a dry frying pan
a few shavings from a fresh coconut, if available
4 tablespoons sweet chilli sauce, preferably Byron Bay Co sweet chilli sauce (or plum sauce)
2 tablespoons light olive oil, plus extra for frying
2 teaspoons light soy sauce, plus extra to season
1 teaspoon tamarind paste (or the juice of ½ lime)
1 teaspoon balsamic vinegar
a good handful of coriander, tough stalks picked off

You've heard the sad story, now here's the happy news. Briskly sauté the asparagus in olive oil for a few minutes until just tender, then season with soy sauce and set aside. Do the same with the shiitake mushrooms, cooking for a good 8–10 minutes to make sure they are properly tender and cooked right the way through. Now simply mix all the ingredients with a deft hand and rain down loosely on to a plate. That's it.

Avocado Timbales with Celeriac, Green Olive and Walnut Remoulade and Tomato and Sweet Chilli Dressing

It isn't often that I want to layer food in this neat, buttoned-up way and there's nothing to stop you from serving the components separately, but it's easy to do and it looks pleasing. This is lovely as a starter or a light lunch with warm bread, the green olive and walnuts adding texture and pungency to the gentle, if rich, comfort of the remoulade. And the chilli sauce adds kick. Not too buttoned up after all.

The avocados have to be absolutely perfect for this: soft and buttery, the outside creamy and a lively green.

SERVES 6

6 small or 3 large, perfectly ripe
    Hass avocados
juice of ½ lime
3–4 very ripe but firm tomatoes,
    chopped
about 8 black olives, pitted and
    finely chopped
sea salt and freshly ground
    black pepper

For the tomato and sweet chilli
    dressing:
6 small tomatoes
3½ tablespoons sweet chilli sauce
2 tablespoons light olive oil
1 tablespoon chopped coriander
    (optional)

For the remoulade:
1 head of celeriac, weighing
    about 600g
juice of 1 lemon
4 tablespoons good-quality
    mayonnaise
6 green olives, pitted and
    finely chopped
2 garlic cloves, finely chopped
1 tablespoon very finely chopped
    parsley
3 walnuts (fresh when in season),
    finely chopped
1 tablespoon grain mustard

First make the dressing. Finely chop the tomatoes and put them, with all their juice, in a bowl or even a mortar. Bruise slightly with a fork or the pestle. Mix in the chilli sauce, oil and the coriander, if using, and set aside.

Next, make the remoulade. Peel the celeriac and cut it into large chunks. Thoroughly rub with the lemon juice to stop it going black. Shred with the shredding attachment of a food processor, or simply grate it on a cheese grater, squeezing out any excess liquid. Season immediately with salt and pepper and add the mayonnaise, green olives, garlic, parsley, walnuts and mustard.

Halve and stone the avocados, then score the flesh with a sharp knife into chunks about 2.5cm square. Carefully spoon them out of the skin and season with salt and pepper as well as the lime juice. Mix with the chopped tomatoes.

In the centre of each serving plate, pile some of the avocado and tomato mixture into a round biscuit cutter, about 7cm in diameter, then press down gently with the back of a spoon or fork. Lift the cutter so it rests on the avocado. Fill to the rim with the remoulade and gently pack this down too. Finish off with a spoonful of chopped black olives. Spoon some of the dressing all the way round and serve.

Note

The ever-resourceful Australian cookery writer Belinda Jeffery suggested I use a small baked bean tin for shaping these, after removing the top and bottom with one of those tin openers that slices the tins open. They are perfect timbale size.

Party Food

A little while ago I catered for 400 Greeks, assembled for the opening night of a film. I had toasted hundreds of small pieces of Turkish bread (a forgiving bunch, this) in my electric griddle. On some I set out finely shaved fennel, marinated in a little olive oil, lemon juice and sea salt. On others, a quickly composed baba ghanoush. Blanched and skinned broad beans mixed with feta, olive oil and lemon topped yet more, and so did wilted spinach with toasted pine nuts, raisins and nutmeg. They were eaten with enthusiasm, passion even.

A group of young women gathered around my table. I wondered if they were interested in my classes, which I was partly there to promote. 'Why would we come to classes?' one said. 'If I want to learn to cook, I go to my mother's kitchen.' We mused about our common experience. None of us, it transpired, had been encouraged into the kitchen by our mothers. On the contrary, I was regularly shooed out and sent to my room to do my homework. It was clearly understood that I and the girls of my generation were being groomed to do 'better, more important things'. But the kitchen drew me inexorably and I would come down with my history textbooks and read them aloud to my mother while she cooked. I liked the reassurance of her presence and the safe female energy of the kitchen. One of the young women, a lawyer, continued, 'None of it means anything without good food.'

Half way through the evening an elderly gentleman with all the distinction, chiselled stature and fine manners of a picture-book hero sidled up to me. 'I love vegetables!' he exclaimed. 'I love fennel. I love broad beans. I love aubergines. And artichokes.' Big sigh. 'And,' he continued conspiratorially, 'I hate meat.' As I was leaving, he placed a gentle and paternal kiss on my cheek. And I loved him forever.

I don't know exactly who started the trend for canapés served in a (Chinese) spoon. It's certainly one way of making just about anything look cute, not to mention good enough to eat. It takes a little planning but it beats watching guests struggling to transfer a fragile

morsel from precariously balanced tray to open mouth. So although I like the laden-table approach much better, I'm happy to pander to this fashion moment for a while. And it certainly dispels the clichéed image of vegetarian food (have I used the word in this book yet? No? Good.) piled in huge bowls, barrack style.

Here's what you'll need for 20 people:

- 20 little cardboard noodle boxes, 200ml or size 8
- 20 coasters, glass or wooden
- 20 pretty teacups, they don't all have to match
- 20 shot glasses
- 20 Chinese soup spoons
- 20 butter-pat dishes
- At least 60 tiny tapas plates

You can look on this whole chapter as one big party and the recipes as ideas to play with. Many of the other recipes in the book can be adapted to suit this format, so feel free.

Mushroom Parfait with Mini Melba Toasts

I have to confess to an almost lifelong commitment to this recipe. I whip it up all the time and continually doctor it to suit the occasion. It has a deep, rich sweetness that everyone comes back for. I like it very smooth, by the way, but it's up to you.

MAKES 20 BUTTER-PAT-SIZED PORTIONS

2 large, black, earthy-looking field mushrooms, roughly chopped
2 tablespoons olive oil or butter
1 garlic clove, finely chopped
1 tablespoon tamari
2 tablespoons brandy
2 tablespoons red wine or Madeira
2 tablespoons ground almonds (almond meal)
140ml double cream, whipped
a fistful of tarragon or coriander, chopped (optional)

Fry the mushrooms in the oil or butter, together with the garlic, tamari, brandy and red wine or Madeira, for about 15 minutes, until the mushrooms are as rich and inky as can be. Allow them to cool, then blend to a purée – how smooth, I'll leave up to you. Then fold in the ground almonds (almond meal) and whipped cream. The tarragon or coriander will add further depth and sweetness. Chill or even part freeze – by which I mean not rock hard but firm enough to allow slicing, or shaping with 2 spoons into cute-looking quenelles (ovals). Otherwise fill some butter-pat dishes and serve with toasts made from very thinly sliced bagels. A little fresh herb and a touch of red onion jam on top, if you have some, will look pretty and taste just right.

Hokkien Noodles with Aubergine Teriyaki, Sesame Seeds and Coriander

Some recipes just stick around, even if they go through different incarnations, and this one has become one of my standbys. As usual, the exhortation to make sure the aubergines (eggplants) are properly fried stands.

If you can buy ready-toasted sesame seeds, then do, even though I ask you to toast them again in the pan with the aubergines (eggplants). Every bit of flavour helps, you see. And serve this hot – it's much better that way.

MAKES 20 SMALL BOXES OR
  6 CONVENTIONAL SERVINGS
900g fresh hokkien egg noodles
180ml sunflower oil
2 aubergines (eggplants), cut
   into slices 5mm thick and then
   into thin strips
2 garlic cloves, finely sliced
6 tablespoons sesame seeds
2 tablespoons teriyaki sauce
juice of 2 limes
10 drops of sesame oil
4 tablespoons pickled ginger,
   plus its juice
1 long red chilli, deseeded and
   chopped to a confetti
2 generous handfuls of coriander
   leaves

Put the noodles in a bowl, cover with boiling water and leave to soak for 4 minutes. Drain and set aside.

Heat the oil in a large pan until almost smoking, then cook the aubergine (eggplant) strips in it in batches so you don't overcrowd the pan – they need to make contact with the hot surface of the pan and go brown and crisp, not just soft and soggy. Add a little of the garlic with each batch.

Return all the cooked aubergine (eggplant) to the pan and add the sesame seeds. Stir over a high heat until the seeds begin to pop, then add the noodles, loosened with your fingers, a handful at a time, until well heated through. Finally stir in the seasonings of teriyaki, lime juice and sesame oil, as well as the pickled ginger and juice, the confetti of red chilli and the coriander, leaving a little of these aside to add as garnish to each filled box.

Variation: Asparagus with Sesame Seeds and Sweet Chilli Sauce
Make half the asparagus recipe on page 152, cutting the asparagus to an appropriate size to fit the boxes, and mix with the noodles. If you can find very thin asparagus (sprue), it looks prettier here and goes further.

Mini Mezze Platter

You can serve these all on one plate or individually in several little dishes.

Carpaccio of Fennel with Lemon Juice, Olive Oil and Garlic

Carpaccio is a borrowed term here to denote something sliced paper thin, in this case with nothing more glamorous than a cheap steel vegetable peeler (one of the few absolute essentials in my otherwise pretty sparse kitchen).

MAKES 20 CANAPÉ-SIZE PORTIONS, OR SERVES 8 AS A CONVENTIONAL STARTER ON THIN TOAST

Take 2 bulbs of fennel, not too large, trim off the brown bit at the bottom and also the stems and fronds, reserving a few of the fronds. Slice the fennel very thinly with a vegetable peeler so you have a mound of it. Mix with a generous tablespoon of fruity extra virgin olive oil, a small garlic clove, very finely chopped (I'll have a word to say about that in a minute), some sea salt and freshly ground black pepper, lemon juice to taste and those reserved fine fronds.

Serve in spoons, on little plates with a dessert fork, or heaped on to pieces of thinly sliced Turkish toast. Some finely chopped oily black olives would make a pretty garnish, as would a little very finely chopped red pepper.

Which brings me back to the finely chopped garlic. You may notice that I never say 'crushed garlic' and that's because I much prefer the neater, less aggressive effect of chopping it. When I say finely chopped, I mean it. I've watched person after person in my classes interpret small and fine as coarse and chunky. I don't know why. And I've held up the coarse lumps of garlic and asked whether they'd want a mouthful of that . . . If you don't think you'd want it in your mouth, the chances are no one else will either.

Courgettes and Grilled Red Peppers with Pesto or Dukka

Chop 4–5 courgettes (zucchini) – a mixture of yellow and green, if possible – into chunky dice. Fry in 2 tablespoons of olive oil until tender. Season with salt, pepper and 2 heaped spoonfuls of pesto. Sprinkle crushed toasted pine nuts on top for added bite. You could also turn to the Lemon and Saffron Risotto with Courgettes and Pesto on page 116 and serve small portions of that instead.

Grill 5 red peppers (capsicums) until the skins are blistered black. Place in a bowl and cover with a cloth so the build-up of steam loosens the skin from the flesh. Remove the stems and seeds, as well as unsightly pith, then slice into thin strips with a very sharp knife.

Place the peppers and courgettes on little plates, with or without small toasts or mini bruschetta. Garnish the peppers with a teaspoon of very good pesto (see page 12) or a sprinkling of dukka (see page 13).

Wilted Spinach with Pine Nuts and Muscatel Raisins

Soak a couple of tablespoons of fat, juicy, Muscatel raisins in a little hot water and set aside. Wilt a bag of baby spinach in a large pan with a knob of butter, then drain well. Season with a finely chopped garlic clove, a little freshly grated nutmeg and perhaps a spoonful of sumac. Then toast a couple of tablespoons of pine nuts in a pan barely filmed with oil until they go golden brown. Bash them with a wooden spoon and scatter them and the strained soaked raisins over the spinach.

Broad Beans with Pecorino

Empty a packet of frozen broad beans into a pan of boiling salted water and cook for about 5 minutes, until tender. Drain, refresh under cold water and drain again, then slip off the grey skins. Dress with 2 tablespoons of fruity extra virgin olive oil, the juice of ½ small lemon and about 40g pecorino cheese, shaved with a vegetable peeler. You can use crumbled feta instead of pecorino if you prefer. Serve in spoons, on little plates or on thin slices of Turkish toast.

Date, Coconut, Lime and Coriander Chutney with Mini Papadams

This is a deconstructed and more modern version of an ancient recipe given by Claudia Roden in *The Book of Jewish Food* (Viking, 1997). In her recipe the ingredients are blended to a smooth paste. I use fresh instead of desiccated coconut and Medjool dates instead of pitted ones and just roughly chop everything together, then serve it on little plates with deep-fried mini papadams. It's very addictive, which is just as well because it's best eaten very fresh.

SERVES 20 AS A CANAPÉ

about ½ fresh coconut, plus the juice
12 Medjool dates, pitted and
    roughly chopped
a large bunch of coriander,
    roughly chopped
juice and grated zest of 2 limes
1½ tablespoons tamarind paste
2 garlic cloves, very finely chopped
½ long, red chilli, deseeded and
    very finely chopped
½ teaspoon sea salt

To serve:
750ml sunflower oil
1 packet of mini papadams

Pierce the 'eyes' at the top of the coconut with a screwdriver and drain off the liquid into a bowl. Break open the coconut with a hammer or heavy pestle. Grate about half to a third of the coconut flesh into a bowl, discarding the outer bark and tough brown skin. Add all the remaining ingredients to the coconut and mix well but lightly, so as not to mash things up too much. Loosen the whole thing with the coconut liquid, but don't add it all at once – you may not need it all.

Heat the sunflower oil in a deep pan and fry the papadams according to the instructions on the packet. They'll take only seconds, so be prepared. Transfer to a plate lined with layers of kitchen paper to drain. Serve the chutney and papadams at once, with very cold beer for a great pre-dinner nibble or as part of an array of bite-sized party pieces.

Wooden Coasters with Toasted Raisin Bread Jarlsberg Sandwiches

All you need to know is that 250g grated Jarlsberg cheese (any grated cheese will do, I'm just having a nostalgic Jarlsberg moment) sandwiched between 12 slices of bread and toasted on a griddle or in a sandwich maker will give you 24 small square sandwiches when cut into quarters. Put a sandwich quarter on each wooden coaster and serve with chutneys and jams.

Thai-inspired Salad in a Spoon

It would be easy to refer you back to the Thai Green Papaya Salad on page 79 and you couldn't go wrong, but here's another one just in case.

MAKES AT LEAST 20 SPOONFULS
OR 4 LUNCHTIME SALADS

Peel 2 thin carrots, then continue peeling them into thin ribbons. Do the same with 3 Lebanese (baby) cucumbers, discarding the core of seeds. Now make ribbons of about a quarter of a fresh coconut, reserving the milky liquid to add to the dressing. You can leave it at that or add a couple of handfuls of very fresh bean sprouts and 2 good handfuls of soaked bean thread noodles (glass noodles). Add the leaves from a bunch of fresh coriander, reserving some for garnish.

Whisk together the juice of 1 lime, about 100ml of the coconut liquid, 1 long red chilli, finely chopped, a spoonful of palm sugar and a tablespoon of tamari. Mix the salad with this dressing and serve twisted on to spoons, each prettily garnished with coriander leaves and a 50g packet of fried onion flakes (available from Asian shops) scattered over.

Thai Red Curry

MAKES 20 CANAPÉ-SIZED PORTIONS

Simply make up the Thai Red Curry on page 136 and divide it between 20 teacups.

Filo Cigars with Carrot and Green Olive Salsa

I'm a little addicted to these. They're like spring rolls except made with filo pastry and I do a version of them so often that, despite the fact that I've put them in an earlier book, here they are in their latest incarnation. Tsatsiki (see page 158) is a great addition by the side.

MAKES 24
500g firm tofu
1 tablespoon tamari
1 tablespoon white wine
a grating of fresh nutmeg
½ teaspoon Marigold bouillon
    powder (see page 119)
2 tablespoons light olive oil
1 large onion, finely chopped
1 garlic clove, finely chopped
1 egg yolk, beaten
2 tablespoons almonds, toasted in a
    dry frying pan and roughly chopped
2 tablespoons plump raisins
1 teaspoon tamarind paste
1 teaspoon maple syrup or a pinch
    of brown sugar
1 tablespoon chopped parsley
1 tablespoon chopped coriander
a thumb-sized piece of red chilli,
    finely chopped
6 sheets of filo pastry
sunflower oil for deep-frying

For the carrot and green olive salsa:
1 large carrot, core removed, very
    finely chopped
75g green olives, Sicilian if possible
    (the organic ones are irresistible),
    pitted and very finely chopped
1 garlic clove, very finely chopped
1 piece of preserved lemon, very
    finely chopped
a good handful of parsley, very
    finely chopped
1 red chilli, deseeded and very
    finely chopped
2–3 tablespoons extra virgin olive oil
sea salt and freshly ground
    black pepper

Crumble the tofu into a bowl, add the tamari, wine, nutmeg and bouillon powder and leave to marinate for at least 20 minutes.

Heat the oil in a pan and fry the onion over a medium heat until it is nicely browned and caramelised, adding the garlic half way through. Add the tofu mixture and fry for 5–6 minutes, stirring constantly, until it starts to go golden and a little crisp in the bottom. Loosen the mixture from the bottom of the pan with a little extra wine if necessary. Add all the remaining ingredients except the filo pastry and sunflower oil, stir until combined, then remove from the heat and leave to cool. Meanwhile, mix together all the ingredients for the salsa and set aside.

Take a generous tablespoon of the tofu mixture and form it into a small sausage shape, squeezing it with your fingers into the palm of your hand. Repeat with the rest of the mixture to make 24 altogether, then set aside.

Lay the sheets of filo pastry, one on top of the other, on a clean dry surface and cut into 4 strips, 8cm wide. Cover with a slightly damp clean tea towel so they don't dry out. Remove one filo strip and lay a tofu 'sausage' at the top of it. Tightly roll it up, tucking the sides in as you near the end to encase the filling securely. Seal the last couple of centimetres of the cigar with a little water. Repeat with the remaining pastry and filling.

Heat the sunflower oil in a deep pan until it is hot enough for a small piece of pastry dropped in to start to sizzle and immediately rise to the top. Place 5 or 6 of the cigars at a time in the hot oil and fry for about 1 minute, until crisp and golden. Using 2 forks, transfer to a plate lined with kitchen paper. Serve at once, piled on to a plate, with the carrot and green olive salsa and the tsatsiki by the side.

Iced Blueberries with Hot White Chocolate Sauce

I can't deny that this is entirely inspired by the iced berries and hot chocolate sauce of The Ivy restaurant in London, but it's so pretty in the shot glasses and so fuss free that I recommend it to you.

MAKES 20 PORTIONS
IN SHOT GLASSES
500g frozen blueberries
275ml double cream
225g good-quality white chocolate,
   broken into small pieces
1 cardamom pod (optional)

Put the double cream, chocolate and cardamom pod in a heatproof bowl and place it over a pan of simmering water, making sure that the water doesn't touch the bowl. Leave until the chocolate has melted, giving it an occasional stir.

Divide the frozen berries between the shot glasses and leave to stand for a few minutes, so they lose some of their chill. Otherwise the sauce immediately seizes on them and spoils the effect. Now pour the hot sauce over, discarding the cardamom pod. Hey presto!

Vodka and Lychee Jellies

These jellies (see photo overleaf) and the other jelly shots that follow are dangerous. You won't feel the kick coming, but come it does. Agar-agar, when you get the hang of it, is easy – so easy that I wonder why anyone ever uses something made from animal bones when they can use something of entirely vegetable origin (seaweed, in fact). But don't make the mistake of treating it like gelatine. It has rules all of its own.

MAKES 20
450ml red grape juice
1½ teaspoons powdered agar-agar
150ml vodka
20 lychees (unless they are very large,
   in which case you may need only 10,
   cut in half)

Put the juice in a small saucepan and scatter the powdered agar-agar over it. Bring to the boil, without stirring at all, until the agar-agar has dissolved. Only then can you stir for a minute or so. Add the vodka, remove from the heat immediately and pour into a jug. Peel the lychees, remove the stone and put them in 20 shot glasses. Pour in the juice and vodka and chill until set.

Serve with a cocktail stick so people can loosen the jelly, then toss their heads back and swallow it in one.

Beetroot and Lime Jellies with Vodka

You will need a centrifugal juice extractor here, to juice the beetroot, carrots and apples.

MAKES 20
juice of 300g beetroot (about 3)
juice of 3 carrots
juice of 2 apples
juice of 1 lime
a dash of Tabasco sauce
1½ teaspoons powdered agar-agar
100ml vodka
2 tablespoons pickled ginger

Put all the juice in a pan with the Tabasco, adding water to make up the volume to 450ml, if necessary. Scatter over the agar-agar and bring to the boil, without stirring, until it has dissolved. Stir briefly, add the vodka and remove from the heat. Pour into 20 shot glasses and chill until set. Serve garnished with the pickled ginger.

Noble One Jellies with Peach

MAKES 20
600ml Noble One or other
    dessert wine
1½ teaspoons powdered agar-agar
1 peach, peeled, stoned and cut into
    20 slices or dice

Pour the wine into a small pan, scatter the agar-agar on top and bring to the boil, without stirring. Stir briefly and remove from the heat. Divide the peach pieces between 20 shot glasses and pour in the wine. Chill until set, then serve.

Dinner Date

When it comes to dinner, I am in a slower, more inward mode than for other meals. I am more likely to set a table, light candles, put on soft music, keep the gathering small and intimate. And because I prefer to eat early, I like things that can be put together relatively quickly, even if they appear more sophisticated or substantial. I would never start to cook a curry from scratch in the evening, for instance; at the end of the day I am less inclined to spend hours in the kitchen. Instead I take a spare hour or two at the weekend to put pastes and spice mixes together and I have a fridge and cupboard with enough aromatics and condiments to make my life a whole lot easier.

Sometimes I'm afraid that all the talk of fast food and quick meals, three-ingredient recipes, ten-minute this and five-minute that, has blinded us to an essential aspect of good eating. Organisation and planning are underused words in the kitchen these days, but they can take a lot of the headache out of cooking. And we are becoming better, more discriminating shoppers. Which is why I include some recipes in this chapter that might at first sight look time consuming — I like complex multi-layered spicing, for example. But when you break the recipes down and plan to prepare some of the components in advance, you'll see that they need not take the entire evening to cook. And when you are well prepared and well stocked up, then spontaneity and instinct can come into their own and you can really start to have fun. Since we all enjoy eating delicious food, I'd like us all to enjoy cooking it.

Cinnamon- and Cardamom-scented Pilaf with Puy Lentils and Fennel Confit

Cinnamon and cardamom are only half the story here. There are also cloves, star anise and fennel seeds – fragrant aromatics to give this pilaf a lovely, lingering complexity.

It's easiest to put the lentils on first and do the rest while they cook – a good 40 minutes, whatever the packet instructions tell you, and I have a packet in front of me that tells me to cook them for a mere 15 minutes. I trust it's a misprint!

SERVES 4

4 tablespoons sunflower oil
3 cloves
3 green cardamom pods
5cm piece of cinnamon stick
½ teaspoon fennel seeds
1 small dried red chilli
1 star anise
1 fresh bay leaf
1 large Spanish onion, finely sliced
    into half moons
1 garlic clove, finely chopped
sea salt and freshly ground black
    pepper

For the lentils:

2 tablespoons light olive oil
    or sunflower oil
1 onion, finely chopped
2 green cardamom pods, cracked
1 star anise
1 small dried chilli
4 garlic cloves, peeled but left whole
2 garlic cloves, finely chopped
250g Puy lentils
500ml water
80ml dry sherry

For the pilaf:

175g basmati rice
2 tablespoons sunflower oil
    or light olive oil
a pinch of fennel seeds
2 green cardamom pods, cracked
5cm piece of cinnamon stick
2 cloves
450ml vegetable stock or water

For the lentils, heat the olive or sunflower oil in a medium-sized pan and add the onion, cardamom, star anise, chilli and the whole and chopped garlic. Fry until the onion is soft and translucent, then stir in the lentils and cover with the water. Bring to the boil and simmer for about 40 minutes. Though the lentils should not lose their shape and texture, they must be absolutely tender. When they are cooked and left in only a little liquid, add the sherry and simmer for a few minutes, adding a little water to the whole thing to loosen it if necessary.

For the pilaf, wash the basmati rice in several changes of cold water until the water runs almost clear, then drain well. Heat the oil in a medium pan, add the seeds, pods, cinnamon sticks and cloves and fry until the aromas are released. Stir in the rice and ½ teaspoon of salt. Add the stock or water and stir once. Bring to the boil, cover immediately with a tight-fitting lid and reduce the heat to a simmer. Cook for 14 minutes or until all the water is absorbed and small holes appear on the surface. Remove from the heat and leave to stand for 5 minutes, still covered.

Meanwhile, cook the Spanish onion. Heat 2 tablespoons of the sunflower oil in a frying pan, add the spices and bay leaf and fry over a low heat for about 2 minutes, until the fragrances are released and you start to get definite notes of cardamom, cinnamon, star anise, chilli and fennel. Then add the remaining oil, raise the heat and add the sliced onion. Cook over a medium to high heat for at least 15 minutes, stirring occasionally, until the onion is soft and a rich shade of gold, closer to teak than pine in colour. Half way through this process, add the chopped garlic.

Once the onion is tender, reduce the heat to low and slowly add the cooked rice to the fried onion and spices, stirring well. The rice will inevitably stick to the bottom of the pan, but you can loosen it slightly with a drop of water. A little extra oil may also be needed.

For the fennel confit:
2–3 tablespoons light olive oil
6 heads of baby fennel, cut into
   quarters, some of the fronds
   reserved for garnish
2 green cardamom pods, cracked
a good pinch of fennel seeds
½ small red chilli (preferably
   bird's eye)
1 garlic clove, finely sliced
200ml vegetable stock
60ml dry sherry

Finally, make the fennel confit. Heat the light olive oil in a frying pan in which the fennel quarters will fit cosily. Add the fennel, cardamom pods, fennel seeds, dried chilli and garlic and fry until the fennel starts to catch and turn gold in attractive mottled patches. Cover with the stock and bring to the boil, then reduce to a steady simmer and cook for 8–10 minutes, until the fennel is tender and coated in a small amount of sticky, aromatic sauce. Add the sherry and simmer until it is reduced to the same consistency as before. To serve, put the rice on a dish, then the lentils, and the fennel prettily piled on top, with a few reserved fennel fronds to add freshness to it all.

And more

My baby fennel had such abundant fronds, all bright and fresh, that I could not bear to discard them, so this is what I did. I put the fronds and the less than perfect outer layers of fennel through a juicer to extract the darkest, herbiest juice you can imagine. Then I melted 50g butter in a frying pan, softened a couple of sliced shallots (golden shallots) and 3 finely chopped garlic cloves in it, and added the fennel juice, all 500ml of it (you can make up the quantity with water if you don't have quite enough). I reduced it over a medium heat to just over half, whisking towards the end to emulsify. Then I added a couple of tablespoons of double cream (an optional luxury) and poured this exquisitely flavoured sauce over the fennel. On a separate occasion, inspired by my initial efforts, I braised the fennel in the juice itself. I do this whenever I have time now.

Port and Red Wine Poached Pear Risotto with Blue Cheese and Mascarpone

Pears and blue cheese go classically well together but perhaps putting them in a risotto isn't obvious. All I can say is that it's delicious, so I hope you enjoy its comforting pleasures soon. There is an art to cooking with fruit, I admit, and this will get you some way there.

A salad of watercress and chicory in a mustardy dressing makes an appropriately bitter foil to this richly soothing fare.

SERVES 4

5 ripe but firm pears, peeled, cored and cut into eighths
175ml port
175ml red wine
1 litre vegetable stock, plus about 100ml to finish
60g butter
250g red onions, chopped
420g arborio rice
110g Gorgonzola cheese, crumbled
110g dolcelatte or Gippsland Blue cheese, crumbled
4 tablespoons mascarpone cheese
a small bunch of chives, finely snipped
sea salt and freshly ground black pepper
freshly grated Parmesan cheese, to serve

Put the pear slices into a saucepan with 150ml of the port and 150ml of the red wine. Bring to the boil and simmer quite vigorously for about 10 minutes, until the pears are tender but still hold their shape and are as pink as an old tea rose. The alcohol should have reduced by about half. Set aside and keep warm.

Put the stock in a pan, bring to simmering point and keep hot. Melt the butter in a large pan, add the onions and fry until translucent. Add the rice and stir over a medium heat until also translucent. Then add the hot stock, a ladleful at a time so that the rice is only just covered with liquid, stirring gently so you don't break up the grains. Add more stock as each addition is absorbed. It should take 15–20 minutes to use up the full litre and then you might need a little more. Add the pears and their cooking liquor to the risotto for the last 5 minutes of cooking. The risotto needs to be quite sloppy, with the grains of rice separate and tender yet retaining a little texture.

Stir in both blue cheeses and some salt and pepper to taste. Then add the remaining port and red wine and a little extra stock – up to a ladleful. Remove from the heat, cover with a lid and leave to stand for 5 minutes. Stir for one final time, then spoon into warmed bowls and add a spoonful of mascarpone to each serving, as well as the chives, some freshly grated Parmesan and black pepper. You could, if you like, save a little of the poached pear and some of the blue cheese to add to each portion as generous completion.

Maltagliati with Dried Porcini in Cream and Brandy Sauce

A good and very simple thing to do with fresh lasagne sheets, this elegant recipe can also be made with the wide ribbons of pappardelle. I don't necessarily suggest that you go to the special trouble of cooking up such a small amount of Puy lentils. However, if you think of this recipe as something to make the day before or the day after a dish of olive-oil-doused Puy lentils served with a tray of roasted vegetables, sweet and caramelised in the sugars released by cooking at a high heat, then so much the better. They do add well-rounded, earthy texture and unexpected flavour. Just reserve a few of the perfectly formed and perfectly cooked lentils (see page 112) to stir through in the last moments before serving.

SERVES 4
40g dried porcini mushrooms
2 tablespoons brandy
2 tablespoons tamari
40g butter
300g portabellini
    mushrooms, sliced
6 garlic cloves, very finely
    chopped
600ml double cream
500g fresh lasagne sheets,
    cut into 4–5cm squares
a small handful of chives,
    finely snipped
2 tablespoons cooked Puy
    lentils (optional)
salt and freshly ground black
    pepper

Begin by soaking the porcini in hot water with half the brandy and half the tamari for about 20 minutes, until they are soft. Drain well, strain the soaking liquor through a fine sieve and set aside.

Melt the butter in a frying pan, add the sliced portabellini mushrooms and cook for 5 minutes. Add the porcini and about half their soaking liquor, as well as most of the garlic. Sauté for 3–4 minutes, until the liquid is reduced by at least half and the mushrooms are tender. Add the double cream, the rest of the mushroom soaking liquor and the remaining garlic, brandy and tamari. Bring to the boil over a medium heat and simmer until the sauce returns to the consistency of double cream.

Meanwhile, bring a large pan of water to the boil, add plenty of salt and then add the pasta pieces. Cook for about 3 minutes, until tender but with a little bite. Drain and immediately add to the hot cream sauce. Stir through the snipped chives and the cooked Puy lentils, if using, and season to taste. Serve at once on warmed plates.

Lemon and Saffron Risotto with Courgettes and Pesto

This recipe only just made it into the book. I cooked it one evening, days before my deadline, and resolved to smuggle it in somehow. Vialone nano is my favourite rice for vegetable risotto but arborio is fine, too.

Courgettes (zucchini) have to be young and sweet if you are going to cook them briefly as described below. If yours are older, fatter specimens, it's better to roast them until very tender and well browned, which can be done in a hot oven while you are cooking the risotto.

A couple of preparatory tips. Have serving plates ready in a warm oven. I don't stipulate this often enough, don't even remember to do it often enough, but it's important and it gives you a little breathing space at the end when you're serving and trying to keep everything hot. Besides, Italian food such as pasta, risotto and polenta benefits enormously from being served piping hot. Also, remember to dice the courgettes (zucchini) before you start on the risotto, so you can throw them together in moments at the end.

SERVES 4

1.25 litres vegetable stock
a large pinch of saffron
3 tablespoons olive oil
4 shallots (golden shallots),
   finely diced
3 garlic cloves, 2 finely
   chopped and 1 finely sliced
375g vialone nano or arborio
   risotto rice
50g Parmesan cheese, freshly
   grated, plus extra to serve
juice and grated zest of
   1 lemon
sea salt and freshly ground
   black pepper
extra virgin olive oil and
   a few small basil leaves,
   to serve (optional)

For the courgettes (zucchini):
2 tablespoons pine nuts
3 tablespoons olive oil
2 yellow and 2 green
   courgettes (zucchini),
   cut into 1cm dice
3 tablespoons pesto
   (see page 12)

Before you start on the risotto, fry the pine nuts in 1 tablespoon of the olive oil for 1 minute, until lightly coloured, then remove from the heat and bash with a wooden spoon to break them up a little. Set aside.

Bring the vegetable stock to simmering point in a saucepan. Remove a cupful of the stock and add the saffron to it.

Heat the oil in a heavy-based pan, add the shallots (golden shallots) and cook gently until translucent. Add the finely chopped garlic and stir through for a minute, then add the rice. Stir constantly until the rice is coated in the oil and looks translucent. Then start the slow, steady addition of hot stock, including the saffron stock, a ladleful at a time, stirring all the while, especially into the sides of the pan, slowly releasing the creaminess of the rice. Add the finely sliced garlic about half way through, so it softens and collapses, and season with some salt and pepper. When all the stock is used up and the risotto is sloppy rather than firm, with grains still separate and with a toothsome bite, though not chalky (the aptly described *al dente*), stir in the grated Parmesan. Cover with a lid, remove from the heat and leave to stand for 5 minutes.

Meanwhile, in a separate pan, sauté the courgettes (zucchini) in the remaining olive oil, briskly shaking the pan so they are tender but still pert and very fresh. Quickly stir in the pesto.

Stir the lemon juice and zest into the risotto. Divide this attractively lemon- and saffron-speckled rice between 4 warmed plates, deep ones if possible, adding a little hot water to it if you feel it's stiffened up. Then pile a mound of courgettes (zucchini) and pine nuts on top, as well as a generous grating or shavings of Parmesan. Swirl a little extra virgin olive oil around and scatter over a few small basil leaves, if you like, then serve without delay.

Fennel and Chickpea Soup with Parmesan

I haven't included many soups in this book, so it's a measure of the high regard
I have for this simple recipe that I include it here. 'You had to come to daggy old
Lismore to find me,' a dear new friend said to me. And the same is true of this
lovely soup, which I found in a quite delightful, unpretentious French restaurant,
Paupiettes, hiding behind an unprepossessing new redbrick façade. Truly, seek
and ye shall find.

SERVES 6

2 tablespoons olive oil, preferably
    a rich and fruity one
1 onion, diced
2 garlic cloves, very finely chopped
1 small potato, peeled and finely diced
1 carrot, diced
1 celery stick, diced
1 fennel bulb, finely diced
2 teaspoons Marigold bouillon
    powder
a chunk of Parmesan cheese, rind
    reserved, shaved with a potato
    peeler or just grated
400g can of chickpeas, drained
sea salt and freshly ground black
    pepper
a handful of finely chopped flat-leaf
    parsley, to garnish

Heat the olive oil in a heavy-based pan, add the onion and fry until soft, adding the garlic
half way through. Then, with a minute between each addition, add the potato, carrot,
celery, fennel and bouillon powder, stirring well to coat. Add 4 large mugs of water and
bring to the boil, then throw in the Parmesan rind and simmer for 5–6 minutes.
Add the chickpeas and cook for 5 minutes, making sure they don't go mushy, so that the
stock stays clear. Skim any foam off the top. Season with salt and pepper and serve as
soon as possible, garnished with the parsley and a good amount of shaved or grated
Parmesan cheese.

A note about Marigold bouillon powder for Australian readers

Made in Switzerland and distributed by my old friend Patrick Tobin, Marigold bouillon
powder is something of an institution in the UK. Every cookery writer in the land,
from Jamie to Nigella, refers to it and it is seriously good. It is available in Australia in
speciality shops, wholefood shops and delicatessens. Ask for it and more will stock it.

Asian Broth with Won Tons

You can buy frozen won tons by the bagful, with various fillings, but none, I think, quite as good as these surprisingly easy ones. You could always make a large batch, since the won ton wrappers come in such thick wads, and freeze them yourself. I used to tie myself up in linguistic knots trying to describe how to make an attractive-looking 3- or even 4-cornered 'hat' for these. Now I just plonk the filling in the centre of a wrapper, bring the sides up and pinch to close in the middle. Much faster and just as nice.

SERVES 4

2 tablespoons sunflower oil
4 shallots (golden shallots),
    finely chopped
250g shiitake mushrooms,
    thickly sliced
1 long red chilli, deseeded and
    chopped to a confetti
1 garlic clove, finely chopped
4 teaspoons tamari
a thumb-sized piece of fresh ginger,
    grated, then squeezed to extract
    the juice, flesh discarded
12 water chestnuts (canned is fine),
    finely sliced (optional)
2 tablespoons sesame seeds, lightly
    toasted in a dry frying pan
4 tablespoons chopped coriander
about 1 tablespoon lime juice
24 won ton wrappers

For the broth:
1.8 litres boiling water or
    vegetable stock
2 sachets of dashi (available from
    Asian and healthfood shops)
a handful of dried arame seaweed
1 tablespoon tamari
2 garlic cloves, very finely chopped
a thumb-sized piece of fresh ginger,
    grated, then squeezed to extract
    the juice, flesh discarded
1 tablespoon tamarind paste
1 carrot, peeled, cut lengthways in half
    and thinly sliced on the diagonal
6–8 mushrooms, sliced and fried
    in a little oil
1 tablespoon sunflower oil
2 large handfuls of bean sprouts
1 long red chilli, very finely chopped
a small bunch of coriander, to garnish

To make the won ton filling, heat the sunflower oil in a frying pan, add the shallots (golden shallots) and fry until translucent. Add the shiitake mushrooms and fry over a medium to high heat for 5 minutes. Add the chilli, garlic, tamari, ginger juice and water chestnuts, if using, plus a little water if necessary to prevent sticking. Fry for about 5 minutes, until the mushrooms are soft with no trace of white left in them. Add the sesame seeds and fry for a couple of minutes, until they pop and splutter. Remove from the heat and stir in the coriander and lime juice.

Allow to cool slightly, then place a generous tablespoon of the mixture in the centre of a won ton wrapper, brush the sides with a little water and bring up into the middle, pinching together to secure. Repeat with the remaining won ton wrappers and filling and set aside.

For the broth, put the boiling water or stock in a pan with all the remaining ingredients except the bean sprouts, half the chopped chilli and the coriander. Return to the boil, add the won tons and simmer for 1 minute, by which time the carrots should be *al dente* and the won tons perfectly cooked. Garnish with the bean sprouts, coriander and remaining chilli and serve at once.

Variations
Deep-fried Won Tons with Asparagus

Place a small, deep pan of oil over a medium heat. When a little piece of won ton wrapper immediately rises to the surface, indicating that the oil is hot enough, lower 3 or 4 won tons at a time into it. Fry for about 1 minute, turning them over with 2 forks to make sure that they are evenly browned. Use the same 2 forks to lift them out on to a plate copiously lined with crumpled kitchen paper. Serve at once with Asparagus with Sesame Seeds and Sweet Chilli Sauce (see page 152).

Steamed Won Tons

You can also steam the won tons for 10–15 minutes in bamboo steamer baskets lined with baking parchment, making sure they're not touching so they don't stick together. Serve with a dipping sauce made by whisking together 100ml tamari, 75ml rice wine, 1 tablespoon ginger juice, extracted from a piece of grated and squeezed ginger, 1 tablespoon maple syrup or a small lump of palm sugar, a good dash of Tabasco and a finely sliced spring onion (shallot).

Sweet Potato Dumplings with Shiitake Filling

These are rather gorgeous little turnovers, best eaten piping hot and useful if you're trying to cut down on wheat. I'm indebted to Christine Manfield for the notion, if not the precise detail, of these.

Don't despair if you don't get them right first time. These dumplings take a little practice and you may need to add a little more flour, depending largely on the texture and wetness of the sweet potato.

Serve with Red Curry and Coconut Sauce (see page 15) and Asparagus with Sesame Seeds and Sweet Chilli Sauce (see page 152).

SERVES 6

3 tablespoons groundnut or
    sunflower oil
180g shiitake mushrooms,
    thickly sliced
2 garlic cloves, very finely chopped
1 teaspoon tamari or soy sauce
2 tablespoons sesame seeds
1 spring onion (shallot), finely sliced,
    including the green part
a small handful of coriander,
    finely chopped
2cm piece from a long red chilli,
    deseeded and finely chopped
1 litre sunflower or groundnut oil
    for deep-frying

For the 'pastry':
750g sweet potatoes
40g tapioca flour, plus extra
    for dusting
30g potato flour
½ teaspoon mixed grated nutmeg,
    ground cinnamon, ground cloves
    and crushed cardamom seeds
a pinch of salt
a pinch of caster sugar (optional)
4 tablespoons light olive oil
    or sunflower oil

For the coating:
175g rice flour
110ml water
juice of ½ lime
salt

For the garnish:
6 small sprigs of coriander
1 lemon, cut into 6 wedges

Preheat the oven to 200°C/Gas Mark 6. Roast the sweet potatoes for 30–45 minutes, until tender. Peel and mash while still hot, then set aside.

To make the filling, heat the groundnut or sunflower oil in a frying pan, add the shiitake mushrooms and fry for 5–6 minutes, shaking the pan occasionally. Then add the rest of the ingredients in the order listed, leaving just a few moments between each addition and stirring constantly. Continue to cook until the mushrooms are browned and cooked right through. Adjust the seasoning if necessary and set aside.

Place the sweet potatoes in a bowl with all the rest of the pastry ingredients and mash with a fork until well combined. Leave the mixture to rest in the fridge for at least an hour. Dust a work surface with tapioca flour and, with well-floured hands, work the mixture into 18 balls. The dough should be soft and pliable, so add a little more flour if necessary. Dust each ball with tapioca flour and flatten it into a circle 4cm in diameter. Place a teaspoon of the mushroom filling in the centre and fold over into a half-moon shape, pressing the edges together lightly to seal.

Heat the oil for deep-frying in a deep pan. Mix together the ingredients for the coating. Dip each dumpling into the coating and fry in the hot oil for about 4 minutes, until golden and flaky. Place on plenty of kitchen paper to drain until ready to serve and keep in a warm oven if necessary.

Serve the dumplings with Red Curry and Coconut Sauce, and a sprig of coriander and a lemon wedge decorating each plate.

Steamed Shiitake and Asparagus Custards

A Japanese potter in Devon first made these for me, many, many years ago, and I was bewitched by their almost ethereal lightness. A good vegetable stock is of the utmost importance here. It has to have a delicacy and sweetness to it, so it's best not to include any strongly flavoured herbs (no thyme, for instance) or dark-coloured vegetables. I go for a couple of carrots, a leek, a stick of celery, at most a mild mushroom and a small onion in a litre of water, with a teaspoon of Marigold bouillon powder (see page 119) if you have some. You can dunk in a sprig of basil and coriander at the end for a couple of minutes, then fish them straight out again. Simmer slowly for about 25 minutes, strain, discard the vegetables and leave the stock to cool. Alternatively, you could use a stock made with dashi, the Japanese dried vegetable stock available in Asian and wholefood shops.

Singing the praises of these delicate custards should not deter you, should you so wish, from adding a touch of spice. A little laksa paste, all hot and fiery, a curry paste, or even harissa or chermoula (see pages 13 and 12), if that's not too cross-cultural for you.

MAKES 8

6 large eggs
950ml vegetable stock
3 drops of chilli oil, or a small piece from a large red chilli, finely chopped
6 asparagus spears, tough ends snapped off
24 shiitake mushrooms, sliced
1 garlic clove, very finely chopped
2cm piece of fresh ginger, grated and squeezed to extract the juice, flesh discarded
a dash of tamari
a dash of Tabasco sauce
a dash of mirin
1 tablespoon sesame seeds
3 tablespoons light olive oil or groundnut oil
leaves from a small sprig of coriander, to garnish (optional)

Fill a wok two-thirds full with water, place a properly fitting steamer tray in it and bring the water to a gentle boil. (You could also use a saucepan with a steamer attachment big enough to hold the cups – cooking them in batches if necessary – or tiered bamboo steamers that fit snugly over your saucepan; remember that any custards in the second tier will cook more slowly than those in the steamer closest to the water.)

Put the eggs, cooled stock and chilli oil or chilli in a bowl and whisk lightly. Do not allow the mixture to get too many air bubbles in it or the custards will be more prone to curdling.

Cut a 10cm tip off each asparagus spear and finely chop the rest. Toss the mushrooms with the garlic, ginger juice, tamari, Tabasco and mirin and add the sesame seeds. Heat the oil in a frying pan, add the mushrooms and fry for at least 7–8 minutes, until they are soft and browned with no trace of white. Add the chopped asparagus and continue to fry for a minute until tender. Then divide between 6 teacups, ramekins or small, round-bottomed Japanese bowls. Place an asparagus tip in each cup and pour the egg 'custard' over so that the asparagus peeks out, leaving about 2cm free at the top.

Carefully transfer each cup to the steamer tray and cover with a lid. Steam very gently for 20 minutes, so that the mixture doesn't curdle. The custards should be silkily smooth, wobble tremulously and sit in the very smallest amount of stock. Garnish with the coriander leaves, if you like, and serve at once for a delicate and soothing starter to a noodle- or rice-based supper, or with Bok Choy and Tamarind Sauce (see page 130) for a light meal.

Gorgonzola Pies with Fig, Pecan and Port Jam

Walnuts rather than pecans are the tried and tested favourite with blue cheese but I live in northern New South Wales, where pecan nuts grow well, so I feel almost morally obliged to use them. Besides, I enjoy them hugely, but you may use whichever is easiest for you.

These generously proportioned pies make a satisfying supper served with Watercress and Griddled Pear Salad (see page 159). I have been known to take the jam out of the fridge and eat it by the spoonful. Oh, and it's great on a cheese plate.

SERVES 4

200g Gorgonzola cheese
3 tablespoons mascarpone cheese
a good pinch of freshly ground
    black pepper
280g puff pastry
a little beaten egg, to glaze
1 tablespoon sesame seeds

For the fig, pecan and port jam:
2 tablespoons light olive oil
100g shallots (golden shallots), peeled
    and separated into segments
400g dried figs, trimmed and
    thickly sliced
150ml vegetable stock
150ml port
3 cloves
1 star anise
a good grating of nutmeg
1 tablespoon sweet chilli sauce
½ teaspoon Tabasco sauce
75g pecan nuts, toasted in a
    dry frying pan for 5 minutes
½ large red chilli, deseeded and
    finely chopped
a handful of fresh coriander,
    tough stalks removed
sea salt and freshly ground
    black pepper

First make the jam. Heat the oil in a saucepan, add the shallots (golden shallots) and fry until they are seductively golden all over and tender right the way through. Add the sliced figs, two-thirds of the stock, two-thirds of the port and all the seasonings. Simmer gently for about 15 minutes, adding the rest of the stock and port as required, so that you have a loose jam, softly caramelised in the figs' natural sugars. Stir in the nuts and simmer for 5 minutes, then add the chilli and coriander and set aside.

For the pies, preheat the oven to 200°C/Gas Mark 6. Mix the Gorgonzola, mascarpone and black pepper together with a fork and set aside. Roll out half the puff pastry thinly on a lightly floured surface and cut out four 5.5cm circles, using a saucer as a template. Prick with a fork and cover with a piece of baking paper until required. Gather the trimmings together, add to the remaining pastry and roll out to make 4 lids, the same size as before.

Place the filling in the centre of 4 of the pastry circles. Brush the edges with beaten egg, place another pastry circle on top and pinch the edges together or roll to make a rope-like seal. Make a small hole in the centre of each lid with a knife, brush with the remaining egg and sprinkle with the sesame seeds. Place on a baking sheet and bake for about 20 minutes, until risen, golden, and crisp top and bottom. Serve at once with the fig, pecan and port jam.

Roasted Pumpkin and Watercress Pesto Pie with Soured Cream, Basil and Walnut Pastry

I wanted a simple pie, thin and elegant but not egg based, with a melt-in-the-mouth pastry. Although it's my usual inclination to layer a pie with several vegetables, each in its own seasoning, I resisted the temptation here. Instead I serve it with Portabello Mushrooms with Sesame Seeds and Swiss Chard with Mustard (see page 154), both of which make natural partners to pumpkin.

SERVES 4–6
850g pumpkin, peeled, deseeded
    and cut into 1cm-thick crescents
50ml light olive oil
about ¼ teaspoon Tabasco sauce
sea salt and freshly ground
    black pepper

For the watercress pesto:
4 garlic cloves, very finely chopped
30g pecan nuts
40g Parmesan cheese, grated
a bunch of watercress, thick
    stalks removed (about 60g
    trimmed weight)
125ml extra virgin olive oil

For the pastry:
150g plain flour
a generous pinch of salt
125g unsalted butter, diced
35g walnuts, finely chopped
6 basil leaves, finely shredded
cracked black pepper
2 tablespoons soured cream

To make the pesto, put the garlic, nuts and Parmesan in a food processor and pulse briefly, then add the watercress and olive oil and pulse again. Season with salt and pepper. It's best used as fresh as possible, but you can keep it in the fridge in a jar with an airtight lid for a couple of weeks.

Preheat the oven to 180°C/Gas Mark 4. Spread the pumpkin slices out on a baking tray and baste them with the olive oil and seasonings. Roast for about 30 minutes, until tender and golden, then slide them out into a dish. Very carefully, with a rubber spatula if possible so as not to break up the pumpkin, fold in 6 tablespoons of the watercress pesto. Set aside.

To make the pastry, sift the flour and salt into a bowl and rub in the butter with your fingertips. Gently mix in the walnuts, basil and some cracked black pepper, then lightly work in the soured cream. Don't overwork the pastry but bring it together into a ball, wrap it in cling film and put it in the freezer for 15 minutes. It will be softer and more delicate than you might expect but putting it in the freezer will make it more manageable.

Preheat the oven to 180°C/Gas Mark 4. To assemble the pie, butter and lightly flour a 24cm loose-based tart tin. Roll out half the pastry on a well-floured surface, ease it back on to the rolling pin, then gently lower it (it really is very delicate) into the prepared tin. Press the pastry carefully into the tin and up the sides. Prick the base with a fork, then cover the pastry with greaseproof paper, fill with baking beans or rice and bake blind for 10 minutes. Remove the paper and beans or rice and return the pastry case to the oven for 5 minutes.

Allow the pastry case to cool (placing the filling on the hot pastry encourages it to go soggy, so be patient if you can), then layer the crescents of pumpkin all over it. Roll out the rest of the pastry, ease it away from the work surface with a palette knife, if necessary, and again roll it back on to the rolling pin. Lower it gently on to the pie, unrolling the pastry as you go, to make a lid (if this is difficult, you can slide the base from a loose-based tart tin under the pastry and flip it on top of the pie). I don't bother to trim it – rough and ready is part of its charm. Use the tip of a fine knife to press little triangular incisions in regular rows all over the top of the pie. Bake for 30 minutes, until very lightly coloured, then serve.

Steamed Shiitake Mushroom and Rice Parcels in Banana Leaves with Aubergines in Coconut Sauce

If you can't get banana leaves (though do try Asian food shops), you can wrap the rice in baking parchment, then in aluminium foil, securing both ends with a piece of string. Soaking the rice twice before cooking may seem laborious but it not only makes it quicker to steam, it starts to break down some of the gluten and makes the rice stickier, which is what you need here. Incidentally, once steamed, the rice parcels can be grilled over a barbecue rather than fried, which will impart a subtle, smoky flavour.

The aubergine (eggplant) accompaniment, traditional in flavour if not in methodology, I owe in part to Sri Owen. However, I roast the aubergines (eggplants), whereas she deep-fries them, and I add ginger, coriander and peanuts to the sauce.

As an alternative to the aubergines (eggplants), I sometimes make a sauce for the rice parcels with nothing more than a little coconut milk mixed with a spoonful or two of curry paste. Or, because I never seem to be without it, I serve tamarind sauce (see page 130). Its distinctive sourness is perfect with the sweet, sticky rice.

SERVES 4

450g glutinous rice, soaked in 350ml warm water for at least 1 hour, preferably overnight
1 can of coconut milk
1 tablespoon palm sugar
a fat pinch of sea salt
1 pandanus leaf (optional)
4 smallish carrots, cut lengthways in half
1 tablespoon ume su (plum vinegar)
1 tablespoon tamari
12 shiitake mushrooms
a little sesame oil for brushing
4 banana leaves
8 spring onions (shallots), trimmed to fit the rice parcels
2 tablespoons sunflower or groundnut oil

Drain the soaked rice in a sieve, return it to a large bowl and pour the coconut milk over it. Add the palm sugar, salt and a pandanus leaf if you can get hold of one, and refrigerate for at least 30 minutes – preferably overnight, which really improves the flavour.

The next day, if that's how long you have left the rice, mix the carrots with the ume su and tamari and leave to marinate for at least 10 minutes. Brush the mushrooms with sesame oil. Unfurl the banana leaves and divide the rice equally between them. Put the carrots, mushrooms and spring onions (shallots) on top, then roll or fold into rectangular parcels. Secure the ends with cocktail sticks and transfer to a steamer basket, one or two parcels to each level, depending on the size of it. Steam for 45–50 minutes, until the rice is soft and sticky and the vegetables tender, with the carrots surprisingly tinged with brown (open up one parcel to check).

**For the aubergines (eggplants)
  in coconut sauce:**
4 long, thin aubergines (eggplants),
  cut lengthways in half
4 tablespoons sunflower oil
2 tablespoons groundnut oil
4 shallots (golden shallots), finely
  sliced
3 garlic cloves, finely sliced
a thumb-sized piece of fresh ginger,
  grated, then squeezed to extract
  the juice, flesh discarded
1 long red chilli, deseeded and
  finely chopped
170ml good-quality coconut milk
1 tablespoon tamari
1 tablespoon rice vinegar
a handful of coriander leaves
a handful of roasted peanuts, crushed
  (a pestle is good for this job)

Meanwhile, cook the aubergines (eggplants). Preheat the oven to 200°C/Gas Mark 6.
Toss the aubergine (eggplant) halves with the sunflower oil, place them on a baking tray
and roast for 20 minutes, until the skins are charred and the flesh golden and soft.
Heat the groundnut oil in a pan, add the shallots (golden shallots), garlic, ginger juice
and chilli and fry for 10 minutes. Add the coconut milk, tamari, vinegar and half the
coriander and simmer for about 5 minutes, until the sauce is quite thick. Transfer the
aubergines (eggplants) to a plate and pour the coconut sauce over them. Garnish
with the remaining coriander and the crushed peanuts.

To finish the rice parcels, heat the sunflower or groundnut oil in a large frying pan
and fry the parcels in it for 10 minutes, turning them over carefully once. The leaves will
brown. All quite desirable and delicious. If you've steamed the parcels in paper and foil,
remove both and carefully lower the rice into a pan filmed with a little oil. Fry until
browned on both sides.

To eat, unwrap the parcels and put some of the aubergine (eggplant) and coconut
sauce on top.

Artichoke and Broad Bean Paella with Aged Sherry

I love paella, with its no-stir, no-fuss cooking, and won't be deprived of it, so here it is with two of my all-time favourite ingredients – artichokes and broad beans. I make it even more often than risotto.

SERVES 6 AS A STARTER,
  4 AS A MAIN COURSE
6 tablespoons olive oil
2 large Spanish onions, finely chopped
3 large globe artichokes in perfect
  condition, firm and bright
6 garlic cloves, finely chopped
250g paella rice (calasparra) or
  arborio rice
150ml dry oloroso or medium
  to dry sherry
a fat pinch of saffron threads,
  dissolved in 150ml boiling water
650ml vegetable stock
200g frozen broad beans
4 gratings of nutmeg
a small bunch of flat-leaf parsley,
  roughly chopped
sea salt and freshly ground
  black pepper
1 lemon, cut into wedges, to serve

Heat a 30–40cm paella pan or frying pan over a medium heat and add the olive oil. When it is hot, add the onions and cook over a medium heat for about 20 minutes, stirring occasionally, until softened.

Meanwhile, prepare the artichokes: trim off the tops and remove all the tough outer leaves until you are left with only the yellow, tender leaves. Cut each artichoke in half and remove the hairy choke with a teaspoon, then cut each half into 3 or 4 segments. Add the artichokes to the onions, along with the garlic, and cook for 10 minutes or so, until the onions and garlic are caramelised and sweet. Add the rice and stir for about a minute to coat it in the oil. Increase the heat to high, add the sherry and boil until the alcohol has evaporated, then add the saffron liquid and the vegetable stock. Bring to a gentle boil, season well at this point and add the broad beans, nutmeg and half the parsley. Simmer for 10 minutes, until the stock has reduced but still covers the rice. Gently shake the pan to help prevent sticking and turn the heat down to medium-low. Cook for another 5 minutes, or until there is just a little liquid left at the bottom of the rice.

Turn off the heat, cover the pan tightly with foil (or baking parchment), and leave to stand for 3–5 minutes. Uncover the pan and serve the paella with the remaining parsley on top and wedges of lemon.

Artichoke and Olive Blini Pan Pies
with Rocket and Radicchio Salad

Probably one of my favourite recipes in the book, this takes all the fear out of
pie making. I never knew there was such a thing, but you learn a lot from teaching.
And I love the fact that these are so very nearly instant yet look remarkably
sophisticated. Cooking them in the pan is how you make bstilla, and you get
a lovely rounded finish to the pie that will make people wonder how you did it.
It helps to have more than one blini pan, so you don't have to make the pies
one at a time.

You could replace some or all of the potatoes with blanched and skinned
broad beans, or even blanched petits pois.

SERVES 6

6 artichokes
½ lemon
2 tablespoons light olive oil
1 small red onion, finely chopped
450g small, waxy salad potatoes,
    peeled and sliced pencil thick
a fat pinch of saffron, dissolved
    in 275ml boiling water
2 fat garlic cloves, thinly sliced
150g meaty-fleshed green olives,
    pitted and sliced to the thickness
    of a pound coin
a small handful of parsley, finely
    chopped
a small handful of chives, very finely
    snipped
1 small piece of preserved lemon,
    or lemon juice to taste
1½ tablespoons double cream
12 sheets of filo pastry
90g butter, melted, or 90ml olive oil

For the rocket and radicchio salad:
150g wild rocket
1 small head of radicchio, leaves
    separated
4 tablespoons olive oil
1 tablespoon balsamic vinegar
sea salt

To prepare the artichokes, trim off the tops to about half way down the leaves. Then
snap off all the tough outer leaves and trim down again to the heart. Cut each artichoke
in half and use a teaspoon to remove the hairy choke. Immediately rub the exposed
surfaces with the lemon half to halt the rapid oxidisation. Slice thickly, putting the
slices in a bowl of water acidulated by the juice from the lemon.

Heat the oil in a pan, add the red onion and fry until translucent. Remove the
onion from the pan, using a slotted spoon and shaking off as much of the oil as possible
back into the pan. Add the potatoes to this onion-scented oil, then the saffron stock,
and simmer for 20 minutes, adding the artichokes and garlic about half way through –
you want the latter to soften, not brown.

Stir in the green olives, parsley, chives, preserved lemon or lemon juice and the cooked
red onion. Toss together in the pan, then add the double cream. Allow to cool a little.

Lightly brush a blini pan with oil. Place the sheets of filo on a clean, dry surface. Cut
each sheet into 3 and pile on top of each other to stop them drying out. Brush the top
piece with melted butter or oil and place in the blini pan, then brush another with butter
or oil and place at right angles to the first. Continue in this way until you have used 6
pieces (in other words 2 sheets, cut into strips). Spoon a sixth of the artichoke filling into
the pan, folding the overlapping pieces of filo over so the filling is securely encased.

Place the pan over a medium to high heat and fry for 2 minutes, until golden brown
and crisp underneath. Then flip the pie out on to a plate and slide it back into the pan
to brown the underside. Turn out and keep hot in a low oven while you cook 5 more
pies in the same way.

Toss all the ingredients for the salad together and serve with the pies.

Salt and Pepper Tofu with Bok Choy and Tamarind Sauce

I used to be strict in my vegetarian endeavour, and fish sauce would not have appeared anywhere in my recipes. But I am less the zealot these days and so have included it in this authentic Thai recipe. However, if you don't eat it, there is a vegetarian 'fish' sauce available from Asian supermarkets. I cannot vouch for its chemical rectitude but it is an option. Otherwise, replace the fish sauce with salt and a little light soy sauce.

Commercial tempura batter mixes, available from Asian shops, are usually very good and worth using unless you particularly want to make your own. Just season very well as below.

SERVES 6
60ml groundnut oil
6 heads of bok choy, cut into halves
    or quarters, depending on size
1 tablespoon sesame seeds
sea salt and freshly ground black
    pepper
finely sliced spring onions (shallots),
    to garnish

For the tamarind sauce:
3 large red chillies, deseeded and
    chopped
4 shallots (golden shallots), finely
    sliced
6 kaffir lime leaves, cut into fine
    strips from either side of the
    central spine
4 garlic cloves, roughly chopped
2 tablespoons grated fresh ginger
150ml groundnut or sunflower oil
100g palm sugar
100ml nam pla (Thai fish sauce)
150ml tamarind paste

For the salt and pepper tofu:
cornflour to coat (or 1 small packet of
    tempura batter, made up according
    to the manufacturer's instructions)
1 dried red chilli, deseeded and
    crumbled
a small sprig of fresh coriander,
    finely chopped (optional)
500g firm tofu
1 litre sunflower oil for deep-frying

First make the tamarind sauce. Put the chillies, shallots (golden shallots), lime leaves, garlic and ginger in a mortar, and pound to a paste. Heat the oil in a large frying pan, add the paste and fry until pale gold. Add the palm sugar, stirring till it dissolves, and the nam pla and allow to caramelise. Add the tamarind paste and stir well to bring the sauce together. Adjust the seasoning and loosen with a drop of boiling water, if necessary, and set aside.

Next prepare the tofu. If you are using cornflour, mix it with the crumbled red chilli, coriander if using, and some sea salt and black pepper. Pat the tofu dry with a tea towel or kitchen paper and cut it into 3.5cm cubes. Coat evenly in the seasoned cornflour. (If you are using tempura batter, mix it with the seasonings as for the cornflour, lightly coat the tofu in plain cornflour and then in the batter.)

Heat the sunflower oil in a deep pan and test that it is hot enough by dropping a small piece of coated tofu into it. If it quickly rises to the top, you are ready to start frying, so have plenty of kitchen paper to hand on a plate. Fry the tofu, in batches if necessary, until it is pale gold and crisp all over. Transfer to the paper-lined plate until ready to serve.

To cook the bok choy, heat the groundnut oil in a large pan, add the bok choy and sesame seeds and sauté over a high heat for 2–3 minutes. Transfer to a plate and drain off any excess liquid. Warm the tamarind sauce through if necessary and pour it over the bok choy. (You may not wish to use all the sauce – there is plenty and it keeps in the fridge for many weeks – so add it slowly at first.) Don't be tempted to add the tamarind sauce to the bok choy while it is still in the pan, or it will continue to weep and turn the sauce far too watery.

Garnish the bok choy with the spring onions (shallots) and serve with the tofu and some steamed basmati or jasmine rice.

Celeriac Gratin with Porcini Mushrooms and Star Anise

Celeriac is an underrated vegetable if ever I saw one, earthy, sweet, and with a sophistication and elegance that belie its gnarled and knobbly appearance. Serve this gratin in large, flat soup bowls, accompanied by warm bread and a green salad.

SERVES 4–6

20g dried porcini mushrooms
a generous dash of tamari
a dash of Tabasco sauce
1 tablespoon brandy
2 tablespoons olive oil
1 smallish onion or 1 shallot
   (golden shallot), finely sliced
1 head of celeriac, peeled and cut
   into thin slices (no more than
   3mm thick)
3 garlic cloves, very finely sliced
1 teaspoon Marigold bouillon powder,
   made up to 650ml with hot water
   (see page 119)
150ml double cream
1 star anise
a few chives, finely snipped, or 1
   tablespoon finely chopped parsley
60g Gruyère cheese, finely grated
   (optional)
sea salt and freshly ground
   black pepper

Cover the porcini mushrooms with boiling water, add the tamari, Tabasco and brandy and leave to soak for 15 minutes. Drain well, strain the soaking liquor through a fine sieve and set aside.

Heat the oil in a large frying pan, add the onion or shallot (golden shallot) and fry until translucent. Add the celeriac, garlic and some black pepper and gently toss them about in the pan for a minute or two, so that the celeriac is coated in the oil, onion and seasonings. Pour in the Marigold stock, bring to the boil and simmer for about 15 minutes, until the stock has reduced and the celeriac is pleasantly tender, which as you'll see can be quite soft indeed. Do not aim for *al dente*, though it shouldn't be falling apart either. Add the porcini and their strained soaking liquor, followed immediately by the cream and the star anise. Simmer briskly until the sauce has reduced to a creamy consistency.

Either serve as is, with the snipped chives or parsley folded through, or sprinkle with the Gruyère and place under a hot grill for about 2 minutes, until melted and beginning to colour.

Polenta with Wild Mushroom and Vermouth Ragout and a Pomegranate and Red Wine Reduction

I can't deny how rich this is – or how hearty, for all the sophisticated ingredients. The huge quantities may seem a little bewildering but you know how these things reduce.

SERVES 6–8

about 30g dried porcini or morel mushrooms
1 tablespoon tamari
1 tablespoon brandy
75g butter
2 garlic cloves, finely chopped
1.5kg mixed mushrooms, including chestnut, button, shiitake, pieds bleus, trompettes de mort and oyster, thickly sliced if large
1 tablespoon soy sauce (or tamari)
a dash of Tabasco sauce
5 tablespoons vermouth
5 tablespoons double cream
a sprig of tarragon
leaves from 5 small sprigs of thyme
a handful of basil leaves
1 tablespoon finely chopped parsley
sea salt and freshly ground black pepper

For the pomegranate and red wine reduction:
85g butter
1 shallot (golden shallot), finely chopped
2 tablespoons balsamic vinegar
seeds from 1 pomegranate
300ml red wine
1 tablespoon finely chopped parsley

For the polenta:
3.2 litres light vegetable stock
800g polenta, quite coarse if possible
2 teaspoons sea salt
60g Parmesan cheese, freshly grated
130g butter, cut into small pieces
a handful of small basil leaves or very finely chopped parsley

To serve:
400g baby spinach
a good knob of butter

Cover the dried mushrooms with boiling water, add the tamari and brandy and leave to soak for 20 minutes. Drain the mushrooms, strain the soaking liquor through a fine sieve or a piece of muslin to remove any grit, and set aside.

Melt the butter in a frying pan over a low heat and add the garlic. Cook gently, stirring constantly, until softened. Add the fresh mushrooms, soy sauce, Tabasco and some salt and pepper and cook over a medium heat for 3–4 minutes, until the mushrooms are soft and releasing their juices. Reduce the heat to low so the juices don't evaporate. Now add the reconstituted dried mushrooms and their soaking liquid. Stir in the vermouth and simmer briskly until the liquid has reduced by about half. Add the double cream and herbs, bring to the boil and remove from the heat. Keep warm.

For the pomegranate and red wine reduction, heat 15g of the butter in a small pan, add the shallot (golden shallot) and cook over a medium heat for 3–4 minutes, until translucent. Add the balsamic vinegar and half the pomegranate seeds and cook for about 2 minutes, until reduced to a glaze. Leave to cool, then strain through a sieve. Return to the pan, add the red wine and simmer for 20 minutes or until reduced by half. Stir in the remaining butter and season to taste. Just before serving, froth with a hand-held blender and stir in the remaining pomegranate seeds and the parsley.

For the polenta, bring the stock to the boil in a large pan. Pour in the polenta and salt in a slow, steady stream, stirring constantly. Reduce the heat and stir patiently for 40 minutes, until the polenta starts to pull away from the side of the pan. Stir in the Parmesan, butter and basil or parsley and season with black pepper.

Finally, wilt the spinach in a pan over a medium heat, cooking it in 2 batches. Strain off any excess liquid, then return to the pan and add the butter. Stir over a medium heat for a minute and season to taste.

To assemble, spoon the polenta on to 4 serving plates and top with the spinach, then the mushroom ragout. Pour the reduction around and serve straight away.

Variation
If you want to prepare the polenta in advance, you can let it set rather than serve it while still soft. Prepare as above, then pour on to a clean surface and spread out in a layer no thicker than 1cm. Leave to cool, then use a biscuit cutter to cut out 5–6cm circles. Transfer these to a buttered dish and lay out in rows, dotting with extra butter and Parmesan. Bake in an oven preheated to 180°C/Gas Mark 4 for 10–15 minutes, until the cheese melts and the polenta starts to crisp up around the edges.

Chiang Mai Fried Tofu and Shiitake Mushroom Curry with Snake Beans and Pineapple

This curry is traditionally made with pork belly and certainly not with tofu!

SERVES 4

500g tofu, cut into 3cm cubes
cornflour seasoned with sea salt,
    coarsely ground black pepper and
    dried chilli flakes, for dusting
1 litre sunflower oil for deep-frying
3 tablespoons groundnut oil
½ pineapple, peeled, cored and cut
    into slices 1cm thick
10 small shallots (golden shallots),
    peeled and cut in half
3 tablespoons red curry paste (see
    page 15), or more to taste
5 cardamom pods, lightly toasted
    in a dry frying pan
2cm piece of cassia bark, lightly
    toasted in a dry frying pan,
    then ground
2 tablespoons palm sugar
2cm piece of fresh ginger, grated,
    then squeezed to extract the
    juice, flesh discarded
300ml vegetable stock, or more
    if necessary
150g snake beans, topped and tailed
300g shiitake mushrooms,
    thickly sliced
juice of ½ pineapple (a juice
    extractor is useful for this)
400ml coconut milk
1 tablespoon tamarind paste
3 tablespoons light soy sauce
    or nam pla (Thai fish sauce)
1 teaspoon salt, or to taste
50g roasted peanuts, pounded

To garnish:
a good handful of fresh coriander
a little finely chopped red chilli
4 handfuls of very fresh bean sprouts
1 head of pickled garlic (optional –
    available from Asian shops)

Pat the tofu dry on kitchen paper, then toss it in the cornflour mixture. Heat the sunflower oil in a deep pan, add the tofu and fry until golden on all sides. Drain on kitchen paper and set aside.

Heat the groundnut oil in a frying pan, add the pineapple slices and fry for about a minute on each side, until golden brown. Remove with a slotted spoon and transfer to a plate lined with kitchen paper. In the same oil, now nicely infused with the taste of pineapple, fry the shallots (golden shallots) until just translucent. Stir in the red curry paste and add the cardamom pods, ground cassia bark, palm sugar and ginger juice. Loosen the mixture with a little of the stock.

Add the snake beans and cook, stirring, for a few minutes until they have begun to soften. Add the shiitake mushrooms a handful at a time. Stir in the pineapple juice to loosen the vegetables, which may be sticking to the pan a bit, then add a little more of the stock plus the coconut milk and tamarind paste. Simmer gently for 8–10 minutes, until the beans are quite tender and the flavours well developed, once again adjusting the consistency with a little water or vegetable stock. The curry should be creamy and saucy but not too thick. Season with the soy sauce or fish sauce and salt, holding some back to add at the end.

Gently stir in the fried tofu, pounded peanuts and pineapple slices, reserving some to add with the garnishes. Simmer for a further 10 minutes or so over a medium heat, then turn into a serving bowl and garnish with the coriander, chopped chilli, bean sprouts and pickled garlic, if using. The bean sprouts will wilt in the curry's heat and need no actual cooking.

Check the seasoning. It should be salty, sweet and sour, with flavours of star anise (from the curry paste) and ginger. Salt 'tightens' the flavours of a dish and must be used judiciously, so add more only if necessary. Serve with a bowl of rice, jasmine by preference.

Thai Red Curry with Pumpkin and Aubergine

For all its heat, this is a lovely gentle curry. I often include it in my Asian spice class and because there's always so much going on, with fourteen people in my domestic kitchen, I have more than once left the vegetables in the oven just a little bit (actually quite a bit) too long so they've come out a little too well browned, a little too soft. The inevitable 'Oh dear, I've overcooked the vegetables' has not stopped me adding them to the curry, which immediately turns the sauce a prettier hue, and makes the curry that much richer and full-bodied, if not quite as picture perfect. Under calmer circumstances, I like to have most of the vegetables in tender, caramelised chunks, with just a few on that marvellous edge of near collapse.

SERVES 4

500g Crown Prince or Jap pumpkin,
    peeled, deseeded and cut into
    4cm chunks
1 aubergine (eggplant), cut into
    4cm chunks
a little groundnut oil
a dash of tamari
2 shallots (golden shallots),
    roughly chopped
6 tablespoons Red Curry Paste,
    or to taste (see page 15)
1 tablespoon palm sugar
2 tablespoons nam pla
    (Thai fish sauce)
2¼ cans of coconut milk, plus
    a little more if needed
3 kaffir lime leaves, torn
2 long red or green chillies,
    deseeded and cut into rings
a handful of Thai basil or coriander

Preheat the oven to 180°C/Gas Mark 4. Put the pumpkin and aubergine (eggplant) on a baking sheet, toss with a little groundnut oil and the tamari and roast for about 15 minutes, until browned but not cooked right through.

Heat a little groundnut oil in a wok and fry the shallots (golden shallots) until softened. Then add the red curry paste and fry for a few minutes longer, adding a little water if necessary to keep the mixture moving. Add the palm sugar and the nam pla, followed by the roasted vegetables, and fry for a few minutes, until they are quite tender. Finally add the coconut milk, the kaffir lime leaves and most of the chilli and basil or coriander, reserving some of each for garnish. Simmer for a few minutes, adjusting the flavour and consistency with a little extra coconut milk or some vegetable stock if necessary. Serve with a bowl of rice.

Mussaman Curry

Mussaman curry – or Muslim curry, as the name implies – comes from the south of Thailand, which shares a border with Islamic Malaysia. The richer, darker Thai curries and the nut sauces, notably satay, are all reflections of the Muslim influence. This is about the closest a Thai curry comes to resembling the curries of India.

It must be said that there is no tradition whatever of meat-free curries in Thailand. David Thompson's fabulous 673-page tome, *Thai Food* (Pavilion Books, 2002) doesn't mention a single one, and though there are modern Thai chefs experimenting, I felt quite free to try my own. It seemed important to keep it simple, without too many vegetables vying for attention. The curry pastes in this book are by and large David Thompson's, with my slight adjustments.

SERVES 4

250g firm tofu, cut into 3cm cubes
cornflour seasoned with sea salt,
    coarsely ground black pepper and
    dried chilli flakes, for dusting
1 litre sunflower oil for deep-frying
2 tablespoons groundnut oil
2 small garlic cloves, finely chopped
400ml coconut milk
200g potatoes, peeled and
    cut into 2cm cubes
1½ tablespoons tamarind paste
1 teaspoon salt, or more to taste
1 tablespoon palm sugar
60g unsalted roasted peanuts

For the mussaman paste:
10 dried, long red chillies, deseeded
    and chopped
1 teaspoon each of ground coriander,
    ground cumin, ground cinnamon,
    ground cloves, ground star anise,
    ground cardamom and ground
    white pepper
1 tablespoon kaffir lime leaves or,
    better still, kaffir lime zest
1 teaspoon salt
6 shallots (golden shallots),
    roughly chopped
5cm piece of fresh galangal, chopped
1–2cm piece of fresh ginger, chopped
7 garlic cloves, roughly chopped

First make the mussaman paste. Pound the ingredients, a few at a time, in a large mortar, starting with the dry ingredients and adding the wet ones (i. e. the shallots, galangal, ginger and garlic) last, working them well to form a soft paste. Set aside. Pat the tofu dry on kitchen paper, then toss it in the cornflour mixture. Heat the sunflower oil in a deep pan, add the tofu and fry until golden on all sides. Drain on kitchen paper and set aside.

Heat the groundnut oil in a wok, add the garlic and fry until golden brown. Add 2 tablespoons of the curry paste (the remainder will keep in the fridge for ages), stir briefly, then add the coconut milk and stir well. Add all the remaining ingredients in turn except the tofu and the peanuts. Simmer gently for 15–20 minutes, until the potatoes are tender but not mushy. Stir in the tofu and most of the peanuts, reserving some for garnish. If the curry seems too thick, you can thin it down with a little hot water. Serve with rice.

Fennel, Pumpkin and Aubergine Tagine

I remember when I was a child, driving along dusty roads from our home in Casablanca to Mannesman, where we had a house on the beach (and I mean on the beach – sometimes the sea would lap, if not crash, against the garden wall), and stopping at roadside stalls to look at tagines and other earthenware coal burners. My parents would buy me child-sized ones so I could concoct my own experiments with the help of Fatima, who worked for us. Should you come across one in a shop selling Moroccan homewares, remember that you have to soak it in water for 24 hours before use. Tagine, by the way, is the name of both the slowly cooked dish and the conical, lidded earthenware vessel in which it is cooked.

I cheat by roasting the pumpkin and aubergine (eggplant) first. This saves a little time, and I enjoy the better caramelisation it gives.

Dessert can be Mascarpone-stuffed Figs in Orange Blossom Syrup (see page 31) or Almond and Rosewater Cigars (see page 180) or, sins of sins, both.

SERVES 6

1.4kg pumpkin, peeled, deseeded and cut into 5 x 3cm pieces
2 aubergines (eggplants), cut into 5 x 3cm pieces
175ml olive oil (don't try to economise on this; you may need even more)
Tabasco sauce, to taste
8 shallots (golden shallots), peeled and either left whole or cut in half, depending on size
8 garlic cloves, 6 peeled but left whole, the rest finely chopped
3 fennel bulbs, cut into eighths
1 teaspoon Marigold bouillon powder, mixed with 750ml hot water (see page 119)
2 tablespoons ground cumin
2 tablespoons sweet paprika
½ long red chilli, finely chopped
a fat pinch of saffron, diluted in a mug of hot water
sea salt and freshly ground black or white pepper

For the couscous:
500g couscous
2 tablespoons olive oil (or lemon myrtle-infused macadamia oil)
1 teaspoon sea salt
750ml boiling water, with a fat pinch of saffron added to it
a good handful each of finely chopped parsley and coriander
2 tablespoons extra virgin olive oil

Preheat the oven to 200°C/Gas Mark 6. Keeping them separate, toss the pumpkin and aubergines (eggplants) in half the olive oil, season with salt, pepper and Tabasco, then spread out in 2 large roasting trays. Roast for 25 minutes or until tender, golden and lightly charred all over.

Meanwhile, heat the rest of the olive oil in a large saucepan (or a tagine, prepared as described above and placed over a heat diffuser). Add the shallots (golden shallots) and fry for 8–10 minutes over a fairly high heat, moving the pan about to prevent burning, until they are translucent and a rich golden colour. Add the whole garlic cloves and the fennel and fry until the fennel begins to brown and to soften slightly, adding a little of the stock to prevent the garlic from burning if necessary. Then add the finely chopped garlic, plus the cumin and paprika, stirring all the time, with about 150ml of the stock. The spices should start to form a paste with the stock and the vegetables' emerging juices. Keep adding the stock a little at a time, stirring constantly. The sauce should become thicker and richer as it absorbs the spices, while the shallots (golden shallots) should collapse and all but dissolve. Now transfer the roasted vegetables to the pan, turning rather than stirring them in. Some will collapse – they are meant to – while others should remain pretty well intact. Add the remaining stock, the finely chopped chilli and the saffron water and keep moving the pan around over a gentle heat. Increase the heat if the liquid seems at all watery or decrease it if it seems too thick.

When you are only 5 minutes away from serving, put the couscous in a bowl and rub the olive oil and salt through it. Pour over the hot saffron water and cover with a plate or cloth until absorbed. Mix the fresh herbs through both the couscous and the tagine and drizzle the extra virgin olive oil over the couscous. Even if you have not cooked the couscous in the tagine itself, it is lovely to serve it in one, warmed in the oven first. Take care, as it becomes very hot very quickly. I have two – one for the couscous and one for the vegetables.

Spinach and Mushroom Lasagne with Semi-dried Tomato Bisque

When I first showed my editor, Denise Bates, my proposal for this book, I proudly declared that there wouldn't be a pasta dish in sight, but then this and the Maltagliati on page 115 elbowed their way in. I trust you will be enticed to find out why.

I understand that the word bisque conjures up images of crab or lobster, so I'm just muscling in on the act here. It's simply that the round, intense flavours and rich texture of the sauce remind me of a classic bisque. Because of the intrinsic saltiness of the dried tomatoes, you won't need to salt it.

SERVES 6

50g butter
450g baby spinach
3 garlic cloves, very finely chopped
300g ricotta cheese
50g Gruyère cheese, grated
500g chestnut or brown-cap
    mushrooms, sliced
1 tablespoon tamari or soy sauce
2 tablespoons brandy
3 tablespoons double cream
four 24 x 14cm sheets or eight 7 x 12cm
    sheets of fresh lasagne (Australian
    ones are larger than UK ones)
1 tablespoon olive oil
sea salt and freshly ground
    black pepper
freshly grated Parmesan cheese,
    to serve

For the bisque:
220g sunblush (semi-dried) tomatoes,
    drained of oil if necessary
25g sun-dried tomatoes, softened in
    a little boiling water, then drained
500ml water
250ml double cream
2 garlic cloves, peeled but left whole
1 tablespoon good red wine
a dash of Tabasco sauce or a few
    black peppercorns
a small pinch of sugar
a small bunch of basil

Melt a small knob of the butter in a large frying pan, add the spinach and stir over a medium heat, until wilted. Drain it of excess water and season with salt and pepper, as well as half the garlic. Leave to cool for a few minutes, then mix with the ricotta and Gruyère, and even a little of the grated Parmesan if you wish. Set aside.

Melt the remaining butter in a large frying pan and add the mushrooms and the remaining garlic. Fry for a couple of minutes, then add the tamari and brandy. The mushrooms will release a wonderful, dark, deeply flavoured liquor, but keep going. Eventually the liquid will reduce to an even more intense juice. Add the double cream and keep on the boil for several more minutes. The whole exercise will take at least 15 minutes, and the mushrooms and sauce should be as rich as rich can be.

Meanwhile, start to prepare the bisque. Simply tip the semi-dried tomatoes and softened sun-dried tomatoes into a blender with the water and blend for all you're worth until it is as smooth as you can get it. Then pass the whole lot through a fine sieve. Again, deep, full-bodied flavour is what you'll get. Transfer this smooth concoction to a smallish pan, add the double cream and the whole garlic cloves and bring to the boil. Reduce the heat to low, add the wine, Tabasco or peppercorns and sugar and simmer for at least 10 minutes, until the garlic is soft, at which point you can fish it out if you wish. Sweep the bunch of basil through the sauce over and over again but don't leave it in there. The sauce can sit for as long as you need – the flavours will continue to develop.

Preheat the oven to 180°C/Gas Mark 4. Fill a large frying pan with boiling salted water, add the olive oil and dunk in the lasagne sheets, one at a time, for 30 seconds each. Fish out with tongs or whatever works for you. Drain on a plate.

Finally, assemble the lasagne. I do this either in a 28cm ceramic tart tin or in the deep earthenware plate of my tagine, which works a treat. Start with a layer of spinach, one of mushrooms, then 1–2 sheets of lasagne, depending on size. It won't harm to reheat the mushrooms before you start, though not the spinach, which would lose some of its spark. Continue like this until you've used everything up. Pour about half the bisque over and place in the oven for about 10 minutes, until heated through. Reheat the rest of the sauce, if necessary. When you come to serve, preheat 6 of those large, flat, white soup bowls or your next best thing. Place some of the lasagne in each one and spoon more of the sauce over and around. Serve at once, with a little grated Parmesan.

Kaitaifi Pastries with Middle Eastern Cheeses

I'd heard of these, I'd seen them, but it took the opening of Mecca Bah in Brisbane before I finally ate them. Love at first bite, you could say. Greg and Lucy Malouf's *Moorish* (Hardie Grant Publishing, 2002), a book I find inspiring from cover to cover, is the source of the recipe itself, but I've played about with it a bit and added my own accompaniments.

Kaitaifi pastry is a shredded pastry that looks rather like vermicelli. It comes in long skeins and is available vacuum-packed from Turkish and Middle Eastern shops.

To serve these as a main course, accompany them with Green Bean and Tomato 'Ratatouille' (see page 159). If you are serving them as a starter, try the Fig, Pecan and Port Jam on page 124 with them.

SERVES 6

180g unsalted butter, melted
1 tablespoon zahtar (a pounded
   mixture of thyme and salt
   or sumac), if available
half a 375g packet of kaitaifi pastry
freshly ground white pepper

For the filling:
1 tablespoon olive oil
2 shallots (golden shallots),
   finely chopped
1 garlic clove, finely chopped
150g haloumi cheese, grated
120g Danish feta cheese,
   mashed up with a fork
1 ball of mozzarella cheese, shredded
60g pine nuts or blanched
   almonds, chopped
30g fresh white breadcrumbs
1 egg yolk
1 tablespoon roughly chopped
   coriander
1 tablespoon roughly chopped mint
1 tablespoon roughly chopped parsley
grated zest of ½ lemon

To make the filling, heat the olive oil in a frying pan, add the shallots (golden shallots) and garlic and sauté for a few minutes, until soft. Remove from the heat and leave to cool. In a large bowl, combine the cheeses with the nuts, breadcrumbs and egg yolk. Add the fried shallots (golden shallots), herbs and lemon zest and mix well. Form the mixture into golf ball shapes with your hands and set aside.

Mix the melted butter with the zahtar, if using. Carefully unfold the kaitaifi pastry into one long skein and ease away half of it, returning the other half to the packet for later use. Divide the pastry into about twenty 15 x 7cm sections, trimming as necessary. Work with one section at a time, keeping the rest covered with a damp tea towel to stop it drying out.

Bunch the strands together tightly and lay out in a strip along your work surface. Brush along the length of the pastry with melted butter and sprinkle with white pepper. Place a ball of cheese at one end and roll it up half way up the pastry. Then carefully turn the parcel 180 degrees and roll the remaining pastry across the other way. You should end up with a fat, criss-crossed pastry ball. Repeat with the remaining pastry and cheese mixture. Cover the parcels with a damp cloth and chill for at least 30 minutes before baking. Preheat the oven to 180°C/Gas Mark 4.

Place the pastries on a baking tray lined with baking parchment, brush with any remaining melted butter and bake in the centre of the oven for 8–10 minutes, until they are golden brown and crisp. Transfer to a plate lined with kitchen paper and serve immediately, piled up high.

Sweet Potatoes Baked with Spinach and Chestnut Mushrooms in Mascarpone and Brandy

I made this lovely bake at the end of a photo shoot for this book, when we had all already eaten too much of too many things, but still, the moment Ian had taken the photo, we fell upon it like hungry vultures. Believe me, if you are not yet familiar with the effect of brandy, tamari, garlic and cream or mascarpone together, you will be hooked after this. And a sweet herb is also good, such as basil or tarragon, or just a little finely chopped parsley.

You could serve this differently, with the sweet potato on a large, deep white plate, the mascarpone-rich spinach in a generous mound on top and the intoxicatingly good mushrooms prettily scattered over. You can even dispense with the Gruyère and the oven at the end, but I have to say that taking the whole tray from oven to table like this made me feel like a proper mum for once, and my friends, who I'm always a little afraid expect only picture-perfect, restaurant-smart food from me, loved it.

SERVES 8

1.25kg sweet potatoes (long, thin ones, if possible), peeled and thickly sliced
5 tablespoons light olive oil
a good dash of Tabasco sauce
60g unsalted butter
750g baby spinach
5 garlic cloves, very finely chopped
a few gratings of nutmeg
2 teaspoons wholegrain mustard
500g mascarpone cheese
500g chestnut mushrooms, sliced
1 teaspoon tamari
1 tablespoon brandy
30g Gruyère cheese, very finely grated
sea salt and freshly ground black pepper

Preheat the oven to 200°C/Gas Mark 6. Place the sliced potatoes on a baking tray and add the oil, Tabasco and some salt and pepper. Mix well and bake for about 20 minutes, until tender and patched with brown.

Meanwhile, melt half the butter in a large frying pan or a wok and add the spinach in 2 lots, allowing the first to wilt slightly before adding the second and turning it over carefully so that the spinach from the bottom comes to the top and vice versa. Add about a third of the garlic and then, when the spinach has wilted, squeeze it gently to get rid of the excess liquid. Don't overdo it though, or you'll end up with nothing. Then add a little more garlic to taste and season with salt, pepper, freshly grated nutmeg and the mustard. Mix the seasoned spinach with a little over half of the mascarpone, then taste and adjust the seasoning. Remove from the pan and set aside until the potatoes are cooked, then spread it over them.

Melt the rest of the butter in the pan in which the spinach was cooked. Add the mushrooms and fry until soft and crumpled, seasoning with the remaining garlic, plus the tamari, brandy and some salt and pepper. Stir in the remaining mascarpone; the mixture should look like a rich ragout. This too, you now add to the baking tray, encouraging the pretty colours of the vegetables beneath to come through by moving the whole thing around slightly with a spoon.

Scatter the Gruyère on top and return the baking tray to the oven for 5–6 minutes, just until the cheese has melted. Serve at once, with a simply dressed salad of young leaves and some good, freshly warmed bread.

Roasted New Potatoes with Asparagus, Oyster Mushrooms and Chicory in Cream and Mustard Sauce

This is quick, easy, elegant and delicious. Try it. To accompany, a green salad of curly endive or rocket with more chicory, in a grainy mustard vinaigrette made with olive oil and a Chardonnay vinegar, may sound like gilding the lily but isn't.

SERVES 4

4 bunches (about 900g) asparagus, tough ends snapped off
60g butter
300g oyster mushrooms
2 large garlic cloves, finely chopped
a good handful of parsley, finely chopped, plus more for garnish
2 chicory heads, cut into quarters
150ml double cream
2 teaspoons wholegrain mustard
150ml good-quality white wine
4 walnuts, very finely chopped

For the potatoes:
100ml olive oil
700g small, waxy salad potatoes, scrubbed and cut lengthways in half
sea salt and freshly ground black pepper

First cook the potatoes. Preheat the oven to its highest setting. Pour the olive oil into a baking tray and heat it in the oven, then add the potatoes with some salt and pepper. Turn to coat them thoroughly in the oil, then place in the oven and roast for 25 minutes, until they are crisp and golden on the outside, tender within.

Meanwhile, cook the asparagus. I do this by lying it flat in a large frying pan. Cover with boiling water from the kettle, add a good pinch of salt and then bring back to the boil over a high heat. Simmer for 2–3 minutes, until the asparagus is tender but still has bite. Drain and refresh under cold water, then set aside.

Melt the butter over a medium heat in the same, still-hot pan, add the oyster mushrooms, garlic and half the parsley and fry for about 3 minutes, until the mushrooms are soft. Then add the chicory and fry for 1 minute or until wilted. Add the cream, mustard, white wine and remaining parsley and cook, moving the pan around over the heat, for a couple of minutes, adding about 2 tablespoons of hot water, if necessary, to keep the whole thing loose. Add the asparagus and heat through so that all – mushrooms, asparagus, chicory – are bathed in the sauce.

Serve the potatoes on warmed plates with a heap of the vegetables and cream sauce, scattered with the chopped walnuts and some parsley.

A Braise of New Potatoes and Shallots with Mushrooms, Fresh Figs, Star Anise and Port

If I had to choose one recipe to epitomise the way I cook, I might just choose this one. It isn't complicated, even though it is cooked in 2 pans, but it has the complexity and depth of flavour that some people think can only be achieved with meat stocks. It's not for the fainthearted (all that alcohol, oil and butter) but I think it's a lesson to everyone, restaurateurs included, who think vegetables are the poor relation, the last thing to receive attention.

SERVES 4
2 tablespoons extra virgin olive oil
300g shallots (golden shallots),
    preferably small ones, peeled
    but left whole
550g small, waxy salad potatoes,
    peeled and cut in half
12 garlic cloves, peeled but left whole
1 star anise
2 cloves
350ml vegetable stock

For the mushrooms and figs:
90g butter
125ml olive oil
200g brown-cap or chestnut
    mushrooms, cut in half
200g shiitake mushrooms, trimmed
½ teaspoon tamari
100ml red wine
100ml port
1 tablespoon palm sugar (optional)
1½ teaspoons tamarind paste
juice and grated zest of 1 lime
a small handful of very finely
    chopped parsley
1½ teaspoons potato flour, dissolved
    in a little cold water
4 fresh figs, cut into quarters

To garnish:
35g pecan halves, lightly toasted
    in a dry frying pan
a handful of coriander
½ red chilli, deseeded and very
    finely chopped

Heat the olive oil in a large frying pan, add the shallots (golden shallots) and fry over a medium heat for a good 15 minutes, stirring occasionally to prevent burning; some sticking to the bottom of the pan will help concentrate the sugars and flavours, though. Add the potatoes and sauté for a minute or two, then add the garlic cloves, star anise and cloves. Add 100ml of the stock and fry for 15 minutes, moving the pan about rather than stirring, so that a sauce starts to form and the vegetables continue to soften. Then add the remaining stock, cover the pan and simmer for 30 minutes.

Meanwhile, prepare the mushrooms and figs. Heat the butter and olive oil in a large pan, then add the brown mushrooms, followed by the shiitake mushrooms and tamari. Fry for 5 minutes, so the mushrooms start to soften and release some of their juices. Add the red wine and port, plus the palm sugar, if using, and the tamarind paste. Cook over a high heat for 5 minutes.

At this point, remove the lid from the potatoes and simmer until the liquid reduces and only a little sauce remains in the pan – enough to coat the shallots (golden shallots) in a golden glaze. Tip all this into the pan with the mushrooms and add the lime juice and zest and chopped parsley, reserving a little of the lime zest and parsley for garnish. Give the whole lot another 2–3 minutes over a fairly high heat so the flavours can mingle, then stir in the potato flour mixture and simmer for 1–2 minutes. Reduce the heat and gently position the figs on top, giving them another minute or two at most, to preserve the exquisite pink of their delicate filaments.

Quickly scatter over the pecan halves, fresh coriander, chilli and reserved lime zest and parsley and take to the table. Serve in deep plates. Polenta, despite its very different roots, goes well if you need something other than bread to mop up the copious rich, velvety sauce.

Ricotta- and Olive-filled Aubergine Rolls with Roasted Bunched Cherry Tomatoes and Yoghurt Tahini Sauce

Roasted cherry tomatoes exploding their sweet juices over the warm aubergine (eggplant) rolls and their rich filling makes this such a pleasurable thing to eat. I make these rolls often, though usually with thin strips of haloumi inside, served just warm enough for it to soften slightly, plus fresh coriander and lemon for a sparkling lift. I like tabouleh, made absolutely at the last minute, beside it. I rarely cater on a very large scale these days but used to serve aubergine rolls as a canapé – dozens of them in concentric circles on a large, round platter. People always loved them.

Choose your aubergines (eggplants) wisely. That they should be unblemished goes without saying – i. e. no soft or brown patches. They should also feel heavy in the hand and have a glossy skin. For this recipe, you need ones wide enough to make decent-sized rolls – think of them as dolmades, if you like. I run my index finger along each one, counting out my slices, to make sure I have what I need.

When I fry the aubergines (eggplants), I have a mound of kitchen paper at the ready as the slices come out of the hot oil, and am always somewhat relieved to see how much oil drains out of them. Remember always to season fried foods while they are still hot – then the seasonings will have twice the effect.

Taste your cherry tomatoes before roasting them. Though roasting will bring out their natural sweetness, add a pinch of sugar to them if they seem too sour.

Serve with couscous or with finely sliced potatoes roasted in olive oil with red onion and tomatoes.

SERVES 6

at least 450ml light olive oil for frying
2 aubergines (eggplants), each cut
    into 12 slices about 1cm thick
juice of 1 lemon
a dash of Tabasco sauce
3 heads of garlic
5 tablespoons olive oil
6 bunches of small, vine-ripened
    tomatoes or cherry tomatoes
    (about 9 per bunch)
sea salt and freshly ground
    black pepper
chopped parsley or coriander,
    to garnish
harissa (see page 13), to serve
    (optional)

Heat the light olive oil in a large frying pan and, when it is very hot, drop in as many aubergine (eggplant) slices as will fit. Fry on both sides until very well browned – at least 1 minute per side. There is nothing worse than insufficiently fried aubergine (eggplant), and no genuine Middle Easterner or Mediterranean will stand for it. Remove and drain on kitchen paper, immediately dousing with the lemon juice and seasoning with sea salt and the Tabasco.

For the yoghurt tahini sauce, combine all the ingredients in a bowl and mix well until smooth. You may need to add a little water to obtain a pouring consistency. Season to taste with salt and pepper and set aside.

Preheat the oven to 180°C/Gas Mark 4. You can place all the ingredients for the filling in a food processor and pulse a few times until combined or, if that seems like too much of a bother, place them in a bowl and mash with a fork. Season to taste with salt and pepper. Take a small amount of the filling in the palm of your hand and roll it tightly to make a chipolata-sized roll that holds its shape. I always make one perfectly sized one and place it in front of me to act as a guide – I do this for everything that entails this sort of mini-production-line effort, as I've seen what happens when you don't. You start off with a sweet-looking little thing and before you know it . . .

For the yoghurt tahini sauce:

180g Greek yoghurt

4 tablespoons pale tahini paste

6 tablespoons cold water

a small handful of parsley,
	finely chopped

1 garlic clove, finely chopped

4 roasted cherry tomatoes, squeezed
	out of their skins

For the filling:

340g very fresh ricotta cheese,
	drained of any excess liquid and
	patted dry on kitchen paper

¼ small red onion, very
	finely chopped

a good handful of parsley (about 40g),
	finely chopped

a small handful of basil leaves, rolled
	up and sliced into fine ribbons

1 teaspoon wholegrain mustard

100g green olives (rinsed under cold
	water if very salty), finely chopped

juice of ½ lime

30g pistachio nuts, roasted in a warm
	oven for 8 minutes, then skins
	rubbed off in a tea towel

2 tablespoons extra virgin olive oil

2 garlic cloves, very finely chopped

Place the filling on each slice of aubergine (eggplant) and roll up. If you are preparing these in advance, put them in the oven with the roasting tomatoes for the last 15 minutes, just to warm through.

Slice the top off each head of garlic to expose the cloves. Place on a piece of aluminium foil and drizzle a tablespoon of olive oil over. Wrap tightly and roast in the oven for 20–30 minutes, until very soft. Place the bunched cherry tomatoes on a baking tray, douse with the rest of the olive oil, season with sea salt and black pepper and roast for 20–25 minutes, until they are softened and the skins have split and gently charred.

Separate the garlic cloves. To serve, place 3–4 aubergine (eggplant) rolls on each plate (on top of the couscous, if you are serving this with it), then add a bunch of roasted tomatoes and a few cloves of roasted garlic. You don't have to peel the garlic before serving but you can if you prefer. Then drizzle the yoghurt tahini sauce over and serve, with a little chopped parsley or coriander on top and a dish of harissa for those who care for it.

Rice Noodles with Four Kinds of Mushrooms

Rice noodles come in many guises – skinny or fat, narrow or wide. My favourite are the ones in sheets, rather like lasagne sheets, which you cut yourself to a size that suits you. I like them a good 2cm wide. They are pre-cooked, so you simply stir them into the cooked mushrooms and stir-fry until they are soft. Easy and mess free.

SERVES 4

6 tablespoons sunflower oil
12 shiitake mushrooms
100g portabellini or chestnut
    mushrooms
2 tablespoons soy sauce or tamari
2 garlic cloves, finely chopped
a good knob of fresh ginger, grated,
    then squeezed to extract the juice,
    flesh discarded
200g oyster mushrooms, any tough
    bits trimmed off
100g enoki mushrooms
1 tablespoon mirin or ume su
    (plum vinegar)
200g courgettes (zucchini), sliced
    lengthways in half and then cut
    into slices on the diagonal
750g ho fun noodles (fresh rice
    noodles)
a bunch of spring onions (shallots),
    finely sliced on the diagonal
1 red chilli, deseeded and chopped
    to a confetti
a handful of coriander,
    roughly chopped

Heat 5 tablespoons of the oil in a wok, add the shiitake mushrooms and stir-fry for 5 minutes. Then add the portabellini or chestnut mushrooms, with half the soy sauce or tamari, plus the garlic and ginger juice and cook for another 5 minutes. Add the oyster mushrooms and cook until tender, then add the enoki, the remaining soy sauce or tamari and the mirin or ume su and cook for a final couple of minutes. Transfer the mushrooms to a bowl and set aside.

Heat the last tablespoon of oil in the wok, throw in the courgettes (zucchini) and fry over a high heat for a couple of minutes. Then add the noodles, separating them out with 2 forks until they are hot and sticking to the bottom of the wok a bit; they should go crisp and golden in places. Return the mushrooms to the wok and toss through. Add the spring onions (shallots) and adjust the seasoning if you need to with a little extra tamari or soy sauce. Stir in the chilli and coriander and serve immediately.

Thai Laksa with Noodles

This traditional Malaysian or Singaporean standby is more commonly made with prawns, but it's very satisfying with noodles. Or you could use the filled won tons on page 120. The laksa paste is the kind of thing you can make in a large batch and freeze, since if you use a food processor rather than a pestle and mortar the whole thing can be done in a matter of minutes. The macadamia nuts replace the traditional candlenuts – still a little difficult to get but worth noting. The fresh turmeric gives the soup its characteristic yellow colour.

Finally, though it's always very appealing to eat something that's freshly made, there's no denying that the flavours here, coconut milk and all, are best left to develop for an hour, before a final blast of heat and the addition of the noodles.

SERVES 4–6

2 tablespoons groundnut oil
1 tablespoon palm sugar, or to taste
1.5 litres vegetable stock
4 thin slices of fresh galangal
1 lemongrass stick, smashed
2 kaffir lime leaves
400ml coconut milk
250g fresh egg noodles

For the laksa paste:
6 shallots (golden shallots),
    roughly chopped
4 red chillies, deseeded and
    finely chopped
1 lemongrass stick, white part only,
    chopped
3cm piece of fresh turmeric, grated
    (or 1 teaspoon ground turmeric)
1 garlic clove, finely chopped
½ teaspoon grated fresh galangal
1 kaffir lime leaf, cut into fine strips
    from either side of the spine
2 tablespoons light soy sauce or
    nam pla (Thai fish sauce)

To garnish:
a handful of Chinese cabbage,
    finely shredded
125g very fresh bean sprouts
a bunch of coriander
10cm piece of cucumber, deseeded
    and sliced into matchsticks
2 kaffir lime leaves, cut into fine strips
    from either side of the spine

First make the laksa paste. Put the shallots, chillies, lemongrass, turmeric, garlic, galangal and lime leaf in a pestle and mortar and pound until smooth (or whiz in a food processor). Mix in the soy or nam pla.

Heat the groundnut oil in a large pan, add the laksa paste and palm sugar and fry for 8 minutes. Add the stock, galangal, lemongrass and kaffir lime leaves, bring to the boil and stir in the coconut milk. Set aside if possible but if not, now add the noodles. Bring back to the boil, just long enough for the noodles to heat through. Pour into bowls and serve garnished with the shredded cabbage, bean sprouts, coriander, cucumber and lime leaves. Eat slurpily.

On the Side

You will find all the recipes in this chapter mentioned elsewhere as components of 'bigger meals', and I do suggest you follow these recommendations. However, it's no accident that these easy and quick suggestions have a chapter to themselves as there isn't one I couldn't make a whole meal of. Even the saffron rice needs only a simple green salad to go with it. I know I must sound like a complete glutton at times (I'm not, really I'm not, and despite appearances I don't spend my whole life in the kitchen) but more often than not I enjoy quick, simple but well-seasoned food, the kind that lends itself as easily to a crowd as to me on my own. And I want to encourage a mix-and-match approach, so do try these recipes in the context that suits you. The same goes for pretty much everything else in this book. I know and you know that if you go into the kitchen inspired you're most of the way there – the recipes will become rough sketches to you, rather than computer-generated blueprints. And it takes a lot for me to say that because actually I passionately want you to cook the way I cook!

Asparagus with Sesame Seeds and Sweet Chilli Sauce

I cook asparagus like this often, whether as a side dish to an Asian meal or as one of many dishes on an informal table. Indeed, this is my preferred way of both cooking and eating. The prospect of a large plateful of anything isn't always very appealing to me, perhaps paradoxically because of an innate greed. I enjoy lots of different tastes, complementary and contrasting, and I am easily bored. Vegetables, as is pretty obvious by what I do, are the central players in my kitchen and, with exceptions, I am not a great one for bakes, and don't even go hugely for pulses and great big bubbling casseroles. I like best to cook several little dishes at a time, none of them madly time consuming, though independently and powerfully flavoured, and to set them out on my 2.5-metre-long dining table, in memory of the feasts and banquets of my childhood. Basically, I like people to feel spoilt for choice.

SERVES 6

2–3 tablespoons groundnut or sunflower oil, with a dash of sesame oil if available

3 bunches (about 675g) asparagus, tough ends snapped off, then cut in half on the diagonal

3 garlic cloves, finely sliced

a thumb-sized piece of ginger, grated, then squeezed to extract the juice, flesh discarded

1 tablespoon tamari

2 tablespoons sesame seeds

2 tablespoons sweet chilli sauce, or more to taste

Heat the oil in a frying pan or wok and when hot, add the asparagus. Sauté briskly over a high heat for 2–3 minutes, till just tender and slightly charred (you may need to do this in batches so the asparagus makes contact with the hot pan).

Add the garlic and ginger juice, then the tamari, next the sesame seeds, and fry till they are pale gold. Finally add the chilli sauce. Toss in the pan for another minute or two over a high heat so the asparagus is cooked in the sweet, spicy sauce, and serve at once.

Portabello Mushrooms with Sesame Seeds

This is a quick, throw-in-the-pan recipe. It's great as an accompaniment to Roasted Pumpkin and Watercress Pesto Pie with Soured Cream, Basil and Walnut Pastry (see page 125), but also very good just piled high on toasted sourdough that has been drenched in garlic butter made with loads of parsley – either as a lunch all to yourself or on smaller pieces of toast to serve as an appetiser with drinks.

SERVES 4
2 tablespoons light olive oil
4 medium-sized portabello
   mushrooms, thickly sliced
1 scant tablespoon tamari
2 garlic cloves, finely chopped
a large handful of coriander, chopped
1 tablespoon sesame seeds, lightly
   toasted in a dry frying pan

Heat the oil in a large frying pan, add the mushrooms and fry over a medium-high heat for about 10 minutes, until soft and juicy. Add the tamari, garlic, coriander and sesame seeds and serve at once.

Swiss Chard with Mustard

Swiss chard in the UK, silver beet in Australia, but it's all the same. Some people feel they haven't eaten unless there's a piece of meat on their plate. I don't feel I've eaten unless there's a pile of greens on mine. I can eat a mound of this with a bit of couscous and a poached egg, or some olive oil-dressed garlicky chickpeas or freshly cooked borlotti beans just out of their pods, and be as happy as anything. I did exactly that just days before writing this, so I'm not making it up.

SERVES 4
2 bunches of Swiss chard (silver beet)
   – about 12 large leaves per bunch
a good knob of butter or 1 tablespoon
   olive oil
6 tablespoons double cream
1 garlic clove, very finely chopped
1 tablespoon wholegrain mustard
sea salt and freshly ground
   black pepper

Separate the Swiss chard (silver beet) leaves from the stalks and cut the stalks into 1–2cm pieces. Shred the leaves roughly. Fill a large pan with just enough water to cover the Swiss chard (silver beet), add salt and bring to the boil. Add the stalks and boil for 1 minute, then add the green leaves and boil furiously for another couple of minutes. Drain, return to the pan with the butter or olive oil and toss quickly over a medium heat. Add the cream, garlic and mustard and heat through. Season with salt and pepper and serve immediately.

Cauliflower Fritters

This recipe is a much enjoyed heirloom from my childhood. Dipping the fritters
into tempura batter just before deep-frying also works very well.

SERVES 4
1 small cauliflower, divided into florets
150g plain flour
a little finely chopped red chilli
½ teaspoon sumac
2 eggs, beaten
sunflower oil for deep-frying
sea salt and freshly ground
    black pepper

For the garlic and coriander yoghurt:
150g Greek yoghurt
2 garlic cloves, finely chopped
a handful of fresh coriander, roughly
    chopped
a handful of parsley, roughly chopped
a little sumac, to garnish

Lightly blanch the cauliflower florets in boiling salted water for 2 minutes, then drain
and refresh under cold water. Pat the florets dry with kitchen paper. Mix the plain flour
with the chilli, sumac and some salt and pepper. Dip the cauliflower into the flour
mixture, then into the beaten egg, and deep-fry in hot oil until golden and crisp
all over. Drain on kitchen paper.

For the yoghurt sauce, mix together the yoghurt, garlic and herbs in a small
bowl and sprinkle the sumac on top.

Serve at once, while the fritters are still sizzling hot.

Saffron Rice

A lovely, golden-hued rice, its grains fluffy, separate and light, to set upon a table
with Middle Eastern and Mediterranean vegetable dishes. Use the best Spanish
La Mancha saffron, if you can.

SERVES 6
750ml vegetable stock
a good fat pinch of saffron strands
3 tablespoons light olive oil
    or sunflower oil
500g basmati rice
3 garlic cloves, finely chopped
2 tablespoons butter or olive oil
60g pine nuts, almonds or pistachios,
    toasted in a dry frying pan and
    roughly broken up
a small handful of parsley,
    finely chopped
sea salt and freshly ground
    black pepper

Bring the stock to the boil, then remove from the heat and add the saffron.
Leave to infuse for at least 10 minutes.

Heat the oil in a heavy-based pan, add the rice and stir till translucent. Add the
garlic, pour in the saffron stock, then add a little salt and stir well. Cover the pan and
bring to the boil, then reduce the heat to as low as possible and cook for 14–15 minutes,
till the liquid is all absorbed and the rice is tender.

Stir in the butter or olive oil, plus extra salt to taste if necessary and a good pinch
of pepper, fluffing up the rice with a fork as you do so. Remove from the heat, sprinkle
the nuts and parsley on top and serve.

Chickpea and Broad Bean Salad

Well, what can I say about this recipe? I've loved broad beans since I was a child and this recipe is a favourite of mine which I first improvised for a catering event about a million years ago. I now keep a tin of chickpeas in my cupboard and a packet of broad beans in my freezer the way some people are never without a tin of baked beans or a packet of peas, and it is in this salad that they are inevitably used. My little boy, who has to be the fussiest eater ever spawned by a cookery writer (and I don't mean anything fancy – he is strictly a pizza boy) actually loves this. It's a little victory for Mum. I'll wager a bet that once you've tried the earthiness of paprika and cumin you will come back to it again and again. Fry some rice, arborio or very softly cooked brown, in an olive oil-rich paste of this spice mix with plenty of garlic and you'll have the basis of another meal – add strips of skinned grilled red pepper (capsicum), kernels of corn scraped from a roasted cob, chunks of well-browned courgettes (zucchini) and there you have it, a kind of Moroccanised paella.

Talking of broad beans and childhood, a friend who came for lunch recently described how he had been brought up by his newly vegetarian single father, whose expertise in the kitchen ran to endless boiled-to-death broad beans. He had loathed them ever since. And then he ate these. I think the whole of Byron Bay has heard about his conversion by now.

By the way, adding tamari to the spice mix isn't some attempt at fusion food or anything like that. I discovered a long time ago that its judicious addition livens up recipes right across the culinary spectrum and gives them wonderful depth and roundness.

SERVES 4–6

500g packet of frozen broad beans
400g can of chickpeas, drained
1 small red onion, very finely diced
2 garlic cloves, very finely chopped
1 tablespoon ground cumin
   (more if necessary)
1 tablespoon paprika
   (more if necessary)
100ml olive oil
1 tablespoon tamari
juice of ½ lemon
a dash of Tabasco sauce or a small
   piece of fresh chilli, finely chopped
a handful of coriander, roughly chopped
1 tablespoon finely chopped parsley

Cook the broad beans in a large pan of boiling water for 7 minutes, then drain and refresh under cold water. Drain again and slip off the grey skin from each bean.

Mix everything together except the herbs and leave to marinate for 20 minutes or so. Taste and adjust the spicing, if necessary. Mix in most of the herbs at the last minute, reserving a little to scatter on top.

Tsatsiki

Nothing very original here, so you may as well focus on brilliant ingredients and listen to a plea about cucumbers. Is there any point to the humongous, waterlogged, anaemic-skinned, plastic-sheathed insipidities we've all made do with for so long? I thought not (and yes I do realise that sometimes it's one of the few vegetables that children will eat). At the very least, look for skinny cucumbers, with very dark, glossy skins, so ridged that they look like lace when thinly sliced. Unless you are able to find the rather rare Asian cucumbers, whose fine skins are almost sugar sweet, it's best to get rid of most, if not all, of the indigestible skin. Even in recipes such as this one, where they have to be grated, I prefer to use Lebanese (baby) cucumbers, which are sweeter and crisper.

Tsatsiki is designed with Greek yoghurt in mind, which tells you how rich, thick and creamy it's expected to be. Serve it with any of the fritters in this book, where it will act as a lovely, cooling foil.

SERVES 4

2 Lebanese cucumbers or ½ large
   cucumber, peeled and grated
200g Greek yoghurt
2 garlic cloves, very finely chopped
2 tablespoons finely chopped mint,
   coriander or parsley (or a mixture)
sea salt and freshly ground
   black pepper

Sprinkle the grated cucumber with salt and set aside for at least 10 minutes. Place in a sieve and squeeze out the excess liquid. Transfer this collapsed heap into a bowl and add the Greek yoghurt, garlic and herbs. Mix thoroughly, then season with a little sea salt – it probably won't need much because of the earlier salting – and black pepper.

Sesame-roasted Sweet Potato Chips

We eat these by the bowlful and never tire of them, with or without a fancy accompaniment.

SERVES 4

2 large sweet potatoes,
   peeled and cut into fat chips
2 tablespoons olive oil
2 tablespoons sesame seeds
a dash of Tabasco sauce
sea salt and freshly ground
   black pepper

Preheat the oven to 200°C/Gas Mark 6. Toss the sweet potatoes in the oil, sesame seeds and seasonings and roast in the oven for about 15 minutes, till tender within and crisp outside, the sesame seeds golden brown and clinging to the potatoes.

Watercress and Griddled Pear Salad

This goes particularly well with Gorgonzola Pies with Fig, Pecan and Port Jam (see page 124). If you want to serve it independently of the pies, you could add other things, such as toasted pecans, or Gorgonzola or other blue cheeses – my favourite ripe Bresse Bleu, for instance. Just make sure the salad has a good balance of sweet and sharp, fiery and pungent.

For each person, core 1 sweet, ripe, but not soft pear and cut into 16 slices. Brush lightly with a tablespoon of light olive oil and a couple of tablespoons of verjuice if you have some, or even a little sweetish white wine. Add a dash of Tabasco and a pinch of coarsely ground black pepper. Set upon a hot griddle and sear for 6–7 minutes on each side, until charred. Dress with any pan juices, a little extra virgin olive oil and a dash of verjuice, Chardonnay vinegar or good balsamic, plus a little sea salt and black pepper to finish. Serve on a generous mound of watercress.

Green Bean and Tomato 'Ratatouille'

I adore green beans but have a horror of them served the way they come in restaurants, even really good ones, all crunchy and swimming in butter, with at most a bit of lemon juice and a few flaked almonds. Try them this Middle Eastern/Mediterranean way instead.

I use the word ratatouille to communicate the fact that this is a rich concoction, the tomatoes quite collapsed, the beans very tender, the onion soft and falling apart, and not just a stir-fry with independent ingredients, barely mingling with each other. I often add sliced mushrooms to the frying onion to make more of this, and serve it with a simple basmati pilaf of well-fried onion and cumin seeds. Sometimes I fold the whole lot through a mass of pappardelle, my favourite pasta, and sometimes I eat it straight from the pan with a chunk of warmed bread. Bread, by the way, never sees my table unless it's been warmed.

SERVES 4
400g green beans, topped and tailed
160ml olive oil
1 red onion, cut into wedges
6–8 garlic cloves, finely sliced
5 ripe tomatoes, cut into quarters
a dash of Tabasco sauce
sea salt and freshly ground
   black pepper

Bring a large pan of salted water to the boil, blanch the beans until just tender, then drain. Heat the oil in a frying pan, add the onion and garlic and cook until translucent. Add the tomatoes and green beans, some salt and pepper and the Tabasco. Cook over a generous heat for about 8 minutes, adding an occasional spoonful of water to loosen the sticky, jammy juices being released from the tomatoes as they break up. Keep adjusting the heat as you see fit, until you have a thick sauce and the beans are tender.

Sweet Things

The French built grand apartments in Casablanca and my aunt and uncle, Tata Titi and Ton ton Sam, lived in one of them. You walked into a square space, all marble floor, with just a large, round table in the middle bearing a vase of flowers or a Bacchanalian bowl of fruit. It was grand and formal and promising of bounty. And bounty there was. Cousins, aunts, uncles, friends gathered there for afternoon tea.

Some time ago I attempted to reproduce one such afternoon for the Slow Food Society in Byron Bay. It was billed as a Middle Eastern tea party, but it didn't take me long to realise that the tea parties of my childhood were much more than this. They spanned a culinary repertoire that took in the influences of Spain, France, Russia, Morocco and England. There were delicate sandwiches of home-made brioche, French *barquettes* (little pastry boats) in their several dozens, containing chouchouka and other fillings. Then came *le gâteau russe*, with its layers of meringue, chocolate and cream; *les fajuedos*, deep-fried coils of pastry dusted with icing sugar. There were light-as-air doughnuts; *choux à la crème*, dipped in glassy, amber caramel, then piled high; *le cake anglais*, a rich fruit cake; *le gâteau marbré* (marble cake); and gorgeous light, crisp, chewy meringues. There was *chloua*, a tricky, time-consuming affair made with deep-fried pastry nuggets held together in a log with caramel. There were dates, which I helped to fill with coloured home-made marzipan or fresh walnuts, and intricate, doll-sized *massepains* – paper-thin pastry cups with ground almonds. And then there were *les cigares aux amandes*, my undisputed favourites to this day, always brought to the table still hot and crisp and drenched in rosewater syrup.

Following is my way of things now, with new pleasures gleaned from my latest (adopted) country and with brush of the past making its mark here and there.

Noble One and Macadamia Cake with Poached Peaches and Nectarines and Noble One Cream

I think the gods were out to help me once I decided to make this cake. In one day, without looking, I came across four different versions: the original Chez Panisse recipe, Stephanie Alexander's, another in a magazine, using Prosecco, and Philip Johnson's, made with Sauternes and, unlike the others, drenched in syrup. Mine most closely resembles his, not only for the syrup but because it contains more egg whites than most.

I love this cake with peaches. They seem to echo the peachy fruitiness of the Noble One – a sticky, amber-coloured dessert wine from New South Wales. Mangoes grow prolifically round here, though, and sometimes, because I like the all-Australianess of it (especially once I have replaced the traditional extra virgin olive oil with the less dominating macadamia oil), I use them instead – about 3 large ones, sliced.

Everything in this cake is done gently. I like to make it in a tart tin rather than a cake tin, to give a large, shallow cake.

SERVES 10

6 eggs, separated
200g caster sugar
grated zest of 1 lemon
grated zest of 1 orange
130ml macadamia oil
2 tablespoons orange juice
140ml Noble One (or other dessert
    wine, such as Sauternes)
160g plain flour
a pinch of salt
½ teaspoon cream of tartar

**For the poached peaches
    and nectarines:**
10 peaches and nectarines
300ml water
100ml Noble One (or other dessert
    wine, such as Sauternes), plus
    a good glug (about 2 tablespoons)
    at the end
4–5 tablespoons caster sugar
juice and grated zest of 2 oranges
1 teaspoon orange blossom water

For the Noble One cream:
250ml whipping cream
1 tablespoon caster sugar
2 tablespoons Noble One (or other
    dessert wine, such as Sauternes)
grated zest of 1 orange (optional)

For the poached peaches and nectarines, place the fruit in a large pan with all the rest of the ingredients. Bring to the boil, then reduce the heat to medium and simmer for 15–20 minutes, until the fruit is quite, quite tender and the syrup is garnet red and sweet with a gentle hint of alcohol, accentuated by adding a final glug at the end. Leave to cool, then peel the peaches and nectarines by introducing the fine point of a small knife under the skin and removing it carefully so as not to damage the delicate fruit.

For the cake, preheat the oven to 160°C/Gas Mark 3. Butter the base of a loose-bottomed 32cm tart tin and line the base and sides with baking parchment (buttering the tin helps to secure the paper).

Using an electric mixer, whisk the egg yolks and half the caster sugar together until creamy. Add the lemon and orange zest, plus the macadamia oil, orange juice and Noble One. Sift in the flour and salt and gently fold into the mixture until just combined.

In a separate bowl, whisk the egg whites with the cream of tartar until they form soft peaks, then whisk in the remaining sugar a little at a time until stiff peaks form. Gently fold the whites into the cake mixture. Pour into the prepared tin and bake for 20 minutes, then reduce the heat to 150°C/Gas Mark 2. Bake for a further 15–20 minutes, until a skewer inserted in the centre of the cake comes out clean. Switch the oven off and allow the cake to cool slowly, as sudden changes in temperature don't do it any favours. I've sometimes left mine in there a full 30 minutes. When you do take it out of the oven, transfer it to a wire rack. Make holes all over the cake with a skewer and pour some of the syrup from the nectarines and peaches over it.

To make the Noble One Cream, whip the cream and sugar until soft peaks form and carefully fold in the Noble One, a little at a time, and the orange zest if using.

Serve the cake, ideally still a little warm, with the poached fruit and syrup, plus the cream and more syrup to hand around. Accompany with a very cold glass of Noble One.

Tiramisu of Peaches with Noble One

A loose use of the word tiramisu, I know, but this is a light, summery version of an ever-popular and supremely easy dessert. It can be assembled in no time and is even better the next day.

You could use nectarines instead of peaches, in which case there is no need to peel them.

SERVES 8–10

140ml Noble One (or other dessert
   wine, such as Sauternes)
100ml apple and mango juice
   (or just mango juice but not apple
   on its own, which is too tart)
10 small or 5 large peaches
12 savoiardi (or sponge finger) biscuits
400g mascarpone cheese
2 medium eggs, separated
5 tablespoons icing sugar, or to taste

Mix the dessert wine and juice together. Peel, stone and slice the peaches. Soak them in the Noble One and juice for 5 minutes or so, then remove. Place the savoiardi biscuits in a flat dish and pour enough of the remaining liquid over them to make them soft but not soggy.

Beat the mascarpone, egg yolks and icing sugar together and add any remaining wine and juice. In a separate bowl, whisk the egg whites to soft peaks, then fold them into the mascarpone mixture. Arrange a third of the sliced peaches in a deep dish, about 25 x 19cm. Place a layer of biscuits on top, then a layer of the mascarpone mixture. Repeat until all the fruit, biscuits and cheese have been used up, finishing with a layer of peaches. Cover with cling film and chill overnight.

Lemon Tart with Caramelised Citrus Glaze

This is a classic tart, which I've included in previous books but never like this, with caramelised lemon slices. When you see the photo opposite, I hope you will be tempted to make it despite the time involved. It's a slow, gentle task. The recipe for the tart was written in England and calls for 5 lemons. In Australia I use the enormous Meyer lemons, and only 3½ are needed.

SERVES 10
250ml double cream
juice and zest of 5 lemons
4–5 cardamom pods (optional)
285g caster sugar
9 large or 10 small eggs

For the pastry:
200g plain flour, sifted
125g unsalted butter, cut into
    small pieces
25g caster sugar
about 4 tablespoons ice-cold water

For the topping:
5–7 lemons, depending on size
250g caster sugar
300ml water

First make the filling. Heat the cream until it just reaches boiling point, then remove from the heat and add the lemon juice and zest and the cardamom pods, if using. Leave to infuse for several hours, preferably overnight, in which case place the mixture in the fridge. Fish out most, if not all, of the lemon zest, as well as the cardamom pods, and add the caster sugar. Beat the eggs one at a time in a small bowl and mix each one into the cream and lemon mixture. Set aside.

To make the pastry, sift the flour into a large bowl and add the butter and sugar. Work lightly with your fingers until the mixture looks like fine crumbs. Add enough ice-cold water to bring the pastry together. Wrap in cling film and set aside in the fridge for at least 20 minutes. Preheat the oven to 200°C/Gas Mark 6.

Lightly butter and flour a 28cm loose-bottomed tart tin. On a floured work surface, roll out the pastry thinly and line the tin with it. Prick all over with a fork, then cover with greaseproof paper and fill with baking beans or rice. Bake blind for 10 minutes, then carefully remove the paper and beans and return to the oven for 5 minutes or until pale gold.

Allow the pastry case to cool. Reduce the oven temperature to 130°C/Gas Mark ¾, then place the pastry case on a flat baking sheet on a half-pulled-out oven shelf. Very slowly and carefully, pour the lemon custard into the pastry case and gingerly push the shelf back into the oven. All this to avoid major spillage. Bake for 50–60 minutes, until the filling is just set but still completely pale. Set aside to cool.

Meanwhile, for the topping, slice the lemons as thinly as you can, using a very sharp knife. Heat the sugar and water in a large frying pan until the sugar has dissolved. Add as many lemon slices as the pan can take in a single layer and cook them gently over a very low heat until they are translucent and lightly caramelised. Lift them out with 2 forks on to a plate. As soon as they are cool, arrange them on top of the tart to cover it completely.

Orange Poppy Seed Cake with Orange Syrup

This is how this recipe came about. It was pouring with rain for the forty-fifth hour in a row after 5 parched months and I called my friend Sharon, to find she had been flooded in and couldn't go to work. She had made Anna del Zoppo's (a mutual friend's) orange poppy seed cake and was taking it out of the oven as we spoke. Of course, I donned my wellies and bombed over there, risking being hemmed in over the creek and bridge that separate our parts of this flood-prone road. I arrived in time to pour the syrup over the hot cake and we ate it in front of an Australian film, *The Rage in Placid Lake*. By the time we finished, the sun was out again for the first time in nearly 2 days. I decided it was an omen.

When I made the cake myself later, I played around with a more restaurant-style sabayon sauce to serve with it, given below.

50g poppy seeds
60ml milk
185g unsalted butter
225g caster sugar
1 tablespoon finely grated orange zest
3 eggs
175g self-raising flour, sifted
50g plain flour, sifted
50g ground almonds (almond meal)
100ml orange juice

For the syrup:
225g caster sugar
grated zest of 1 orange
grated zest of 1 lime
70ml water
150ml orange juice

Butter a kugelhopf tin (you will find the cake cooks more thoroughly in this than in a conventional tin) and preheat the oven to 180°C/Gas Mark 4. Combine the poppy seeds and milk in a bowl and leave to stand for 20 minutes.

Beat the butter, sugar and orange zest together until light and fluffy, then beat in the eggs, one at a time, until well combined. Stir in the flours, ground almonds (almond meal), orange juice and the poppy seeds and milk. Pour into the prepared tin and bake for 55 minutes or until a skewer inserted in the centre comes out clean. Remove from the oven and turn out on to a wire rack.

For the syrup, put the sugar, orange and lime zest and water in a pan and heat gently until the sugar dissolves. Simmer until it turns to a syrup, then add the orange juice and briefly bring back to the boil. Pour the hot syrup over the hot cake and eat at once, with crème fraîche, cream, ice cream or Greek yoghurt – or, of course, the delicious sauce opposite.

Orange and Star Anise Sabayon

This is a lovely, rich alternative to serve with the Orange Poppy Seed Cake opposite, and immediately elevates it from afternoon-tea cake to smart dessert. Indeed, it would work well with almost any of the cakes in this book or as a dessert in its own right with poached peaches and nectarines (see page 162) or Caramelised Kumquats (see page 179).

The method is full of cautionary warnings but don't let that make you think it is difficult to do because it isn't. You can replace the Cointreau or Grand Marnier with a dessert wine such as Sauternes or Noble One for a really fine alternative.

8 large egg yolks
75g caster sugar
1 star anise
250ml Cointreau or Grand Marnier
grated zest of 1 orange

Place the egg yolks, sugar, star anise and Cointreau or Grand Marnier in a heatproof glass or copper bowl and place it over a pan of gently simmering water, making sure the water is not touching the base of the bowl. Quickly and continuously whisk with a large balloon whisk or a hand-held electric beater until the mixture becomes foamy and thick – it should be thick enough to leave a trail on the surface when dropped from the whisk. Do not let the water boil or the eggs overheat; if you sense the mixture becoming hotter than body heat, remove the bowl from the pan for a minute and let it cool down slightly before continuing.

When the sabayon is cool, remove from the heat. Partly fill the sink with cold water and place the bowl in it. Continue to whisk until the mixture is room temperature. Only then add the orange zest. Fish out the star anise and serve the sabayon at once.

Chocolate Hazelnut Cake with Frangelico Cream and Hazelnut Praline

This is a gorgeous cake, usually made with ground almonds (almond meal), which of course you can use if you like. Chocolate and hazelnuts are an incomparable match, though, and you could serve this with a shot glass of ice-cold Frangelico, the hazelnut-flavoured liqueur.

SERVES 8
110g hazelnuts
150g dark chocolate
    (70 per cent cocoa solids)
150g unsalted butter
35g cocoa powder,
    plus extra to serve, if liked
80ml hot water
275g dark brown sugar
4 eggs, separated

For the hazelnut praline:
250g hazelnuts
225g caster sugar
110ml water

For the Frangelico cream:
250ml whipping cream
2 tablespoons icing sugar
1 tablespoon Frangelico liqueur

Butter a round, deep, 20cm cake tin and line the sides and base with baking parchment. Preheat the oven to 180°C/Gas Mark 4.

Lightly toast the hazelnuts for the cake and the praline in a dry frying pan over a low heat for 8–10 minutes, then leave to cool. Put them in a tea towel and rub off the skins. Grind the hazelnuts for the cake in a food processor and roughly chop the ones for the praline. Set aside.

Put the chocolate and butter in a bowl placed over a pan of gently simmering water and leave until melted. Remove from the heat. Combine the cocoa powder and hot water in a large bowl and stir until smooth. Then add the melted chocolate and butter, sugar and ground hazelnuts and stir until combined. Add the egg yolks, one at a time, stirring well after each addition.

In a separate bowl, whisk the egg whites until they form soft peaks. Fold them gently into the chocolate mixture in 2 batches. Pour the mixture into the prepared tin and bake for about 1¾ hours. When the cake is done it will be crisp and friable on top, a little like meringue, and soft and slightly gooey inside. Remove from the oven and leave to cool in the tin.

For the hazelnut praline, spread the nuts out on a baking tray lined with baking parchment. Put the sugar and water in a small, heavy-based saucepan and heat gently, stirring occasionally, until the sugar has dissolved. Raise the heat and boil without stirring until it turns a deep amber colour. Pour this caramel immediately over the nuts and allow to harden to a glassy crisp. Break into shards. (The praline can be stored in an airtight jar and use as required; it's also great with ice cream, either as is or roughly pulverised in a food processor.)

For the Frangelico cream, put the cream and icing sugar in a bowl and whip until the cream forms soft peaks, then fold in the Frangelico.

Turn the cake out of the tin and dust with cocoa powder, if you like. Serve with the Frangelico cream and hazelnut praline. To get good clean slices, you will need to cut the cake with a hot knife (i. e. one that's been dipped in very hot water and then dried).

Middle Eastern Pistachio and Orange Cake with a Chocolate and Pistachio Top

The more traditional almond and orange cake is everywhere these days and I get a little tired of it, so I thought I'd ring the changes. I've made this version especially moist and added chocolate because I'm an addict, but you don't have to. It's a well-established Passover cake, by the way. My mother makes it every year (as probably does every observant Jewish woman in the world) because of its lack of flour.

2 large oranges
6 eggs
250g caster sugar
250g ground pistachio nuts
1 teaspoon baking powder

For the syrup:
225g caster sugar
juice and grated zest of 1 orange
125ml water
a sprig of coriander (optional)
3 black peppercorns (optional)
4 cardamom pods
1 teaspoon lemon juice
½ teaspoon orange blossom water

For the chocolate and pistachio top:
50g pistachio nuts
150g dark chocolate
75g unsalted butter
1 tablespoon maple syrup

Preheat the oven to 180°C/Gas Mark 4. Butter and flour a 25cm springform cake tin or line it with baking parchment (always my preference – no nasty surprises when you try to turn the cake out).

Put the oranges in a large pan, cover with water and bring to the boil. Cover and simmer for 2 hours, adding more water to cover if necessary. Allow to cool, then remove the pips and roughly chop the oranges, skin and all. Put them in a blender or food processor and process to a pulp.

Using an electric mixer, beat the eggs and sugar together until they are pale and thick. Rain in the ground pistachios and baking powder and keep beating for a few seconds. Then stop, add the puréed oranges and beat again for a few more seconds until they are well mixed in. Transfer the mixture to the prepared cake tin and bake for a good hour, covering with a piece of baking parchment about three-quarters of the way through to stop it going too dark on top. The cake is done when a skewer inserted in the centre comes out clean.

Meanwhile, make the syrup. Put all the ingredients in a pan and bring to the boil. Simmer for 10 minutes, then strain. When the cake is done, leave it in the tin to cool, then gently turn it out. Pierce all over with a skewer and pour over the syrup.
For the topping, preheat the oven to its lowest setting. Spread the pistachios out on a baking tray, place in the oven and leave for about 20 minutes; they shouldn't colour. Skin them by rubbing them in a clean tea towel, then chop roughly. Put the nuts and all the rest of the topping ingredients in a bowl placed over a pan of simmering water, making sure the water doesn't touch the bowl. Leave until the chocolate and butter have melted, then stir well to amalgamate the ingredients into a smooth, silky, shiny ganache, studded with pistachios.

Place the cake on a large, round plate and pour over the topping while it is still hot, swivelling the plate about gently to achieve an even covering.

Crème Brûlée with Lemon Myrtle

You know how it is. Every now and again you come across something new and develop a veritable love affair with it. Lemon myrtle has become my new rosewater. I absolutely love it. It started when someone in my cookery classes told me that he had lemon myrtle trees on his property. A few days later, he placed a huge bunch of it on my doorstep. I am ashamed to say that it remained in a wooden bowl for weeks (months, actually), drying to a crisp. Although I missed out on using it fresh in curries, as he had suggested, I now found myself pounding the whole lot, stripped of its bark, in my pestle and mortar to as fine a powder as I could and sifting it through a sieve to remove the debris.

And then it started. The obsession. First this crème brûlée. Then a hollandaise sauce (see page 24), then in couscous (see page 138), in salad dressings, then addictively in macadamia oil and in ice cream. And I'm sure it's not over yet.

SERVES 8
150g caster sugar
10 egg yolks
2 teaspoons ground lemon myrtle
100ml milk
900ml double cream
150g demerara sugar

Preheat the oven to 140°C/Gas Mark 1. Using an electric mixer on a low speed, beat the caster sugar with the egg yolks until thick and creamy. Mix the lemon myrtle with a little of the milk and stir well to remove any lumps – you may have to strain it through a sieve. Put the remaining milk and the cream in a pan with the lemon myrtle paste, stirring it in thoroughly, and heat almost to boiling point, taking care that the mixture does not boil. With the mixer turned even lower, gradually add the milk and cream to the beaten egg mixture. Pour into a large ovenproof dish (I use one 32 x 13cm, about 5cm deep) and place it in a *bain marie* – basically a large roasting tin one-third filled with water. Bake for about 1 hour, until set. Place in the fridge to chill and firm to a thick, spoonable cream.

When ready to serve, sprinkle the demerara sugar evenly over the surface and caramelise under a very hot grill or, better still, with a blowtorch.

Watch carefully that the sugar does not burn. When it has set to a luminescent amber-coloured glass, wait a few minutes for it to cool, then serve.

Just a word of warning. The ground-up lemon myrtle will turn the crème brûlée a little grey, but don't let that bother you.

Lemon Myrtle Shortbreads

My friend Victoria almost always visits with a little cellophane bag of shortbreads, all beribboned and impressive looking. What's more, she bakes a tray of them every Sunday – different flavours, different shapes – and takes a bag to work on Monday morning. And you thought people like that only existed in cookery books and 'lifestyle' magazines.

As a breakfast biscuit eater, I can't think of anything better than these super-crumbly, melt-in-the mouth shortbreads. Below I give you two alternative flavourings – one ever so English, the other purely Australian. If you are making the lavender version, try to find Provençal lavender.

MAKES ABOUT 30
300g plain flour
2 tablespoons rice flour
55g icing sugar
2 tablespoons ground lemon myrtle
   (or 2 tablespoons ground dried
   lavender flowers)
250g butter, cut into cubes

Preheat the oven to 160°C/Gas Mark 3. Line 2 baking trays with baking parchment. Sift the plain flour and rice flour into a bowl. The lighter the flour, the more air in it, the crumblier the shortbread. Stir in the icing sugar and ground lemon myrtle, then rub in the butter with your fingertips until the mixture resembles breadcrumbs. Press together to make a dough.

Turn out on to a lightly floured surface and knead gently for a moment. Divide the dough in half and roll each piece out to about 7mm thick. It helps to roll it out between 2 sheets of baking parchment to prevent it sticking. Cut out with a fluted 6cm biscuit cutter and place on lightly buttered and floured baking trays. Bake for 10–15 minutes, until golden, then remove from the oven and leave on the trays for 5 minutes. Transfer to a wire rack to cool. Store in an airtight container for up to a month (or is that wishful thinking?).

Portuguese Custard Tarts
with a Moorish Twist of Rosewater

Either the recipe for this is a closely guarded secret or I've been very unlucky.
I have tried recipe after recipe, each time with disappointing results – curdled
custard, insufficiently flaky pastry, inauthentic ingredients (custard powder –
purlease!). But I've persevered because I think these count amongst the most
gorgeous of little cakes. So, for some discoveries: most Australian milk isn't quite
rich enough to achieve a custard that will take to being baked without adding
unpleasant amounts of cornflour. Hence the addition of double cream. My friend
of Portuguese descent (half Portuguese, half Macaon – how's that for exotic?)
confirms this and tells how her mother, living in Sydney, always insisted that the
quality of the milk made all the difference. The pastry is flaky and you have to make
it yourself – no short cuts, no puff pastry imitation. You want the real thing, don't
you? And once you've got it, you can allow yourself a little fancy – the rosewater,
a fine and noble thing here. Which makes the scattering of petals plucked from
2 pale pink roses seem appropriate: dip them first in a little lightly whisked
egg white, then cover in a soft shower of caster sugar until they dry and set
to a delicate, crystallised crisp.

I am grateful to Lulu Grimes for reminding me of another tip that adds
authenticity to this recipe. The Portuguese roll out the pastry and then roll it
up tightly into a Swiss roll. They then slice it thinly (as if making biscuits) and
roll out each piece separately before lining the moulds with them. This gives
the pastry its characteristic unravelling like a spiral when baked.

MAKES 18
180g caster sugar
180ml water
4 tablespoons cornflour
440ml full-fat milk
560ml double cream
10 large egg yolks
4 teaspoons rosewater

For the sweet flaky pastry:
250g plain flour
2 tablespoons caster sugar
100g butter, cut into small cubes
150ml cold water
150g soft, pliable butter, diced

First make the pastry. Sift the flour into a bowl, stir in the caster sugar and rub in the first lot of butter until the mixture resembles fine crumbs. Mix in the cold water until you have a smooth, soft paste. Roll it lightly into a ball, cover with cling film and chill for 15 minutes.

Roll out the pastry on a lightly floured surface until it is 45cm long. Spread two-thirds of the soft butter over two-thirds of the pastry and fold the unbuttered third over. Spread the remaining butter over this and then fold again to encase the butter. Wrap in cling film and chill for 15 minutes.

Roll out the pastry, giving it two 90-degree turns, until it is 45cm long and 15cm wide. Then fold it in 3. Turn this parcel 90 degrees and then roll and fold as before. Wrap in cling film and leave to rest in the fridge for a final 10 minutes.

Lightly butter and flour 18 cups of 3 muffin tins. On a lightly floured surface, roll out the pastry to about 3mm thick and cut out rounds to fit the muffin cups (I use a saucer and cut around it with a small, sharp knife). Chill while you make the filling. Preheat the oven to 180°C/Gas Mark 4. To make the filling, put the sugar and water in a small saucepan and stir over a gentle heat until the sugar has dissolved. Raise the heat and boil vigorously, without stirring, until the mixture is syrupy but not coloured. Remove from the heat and set aside.

Dissolve the cornflour in a little of the milk. Heat the rest of the milk with the double cream until it reaches boiling point, then immediately remove from the heat. In a large bowl, beat the egg yolks until thick. Mix in the hot milk, sugar syrup and dissolved cornflour. Pour this custard into a clean saucepan and stir over a low heat until it comes to the boil and thickens. Stir in the rosewater and once again remove from the heat immediately, so it doesn't burn or curdle.

Pour the mixture into the prepared tins and bake for 20 minutes in the preheated oven, by which time the pastry will be as flaky as you could hope for, the custard set and the top characteristically browned in mottled patches. Allow to cool, then serve with crystallised rose petals, if liked.

Date and Caramelised Walnut Crème Brûlée Tart

I have long loved crème brûlée tarts. Years ago, I used to go to a gorgeous deli in Primrose Hill in London, specifically for their raspberry and crème brûlée tart. When they closed down I began to make my own, with raspberries and also with fresh figs. On a recent trip to Sydney I was encouraged by several people to try the date brûlée tart at Yellow, which got me thinking on the subject again. One step, two steps and here you are: caramelised walnuts, making a sharp contrast to all that divine sweetness, and a sticky Medjool date on top.

Adding lime zest to the walnuts may seem, if not wasteful, then superfluous but my father's words instruct my cooking. '*Il faut que le goût soit rond* [the flavour should be well rounded],' he used to say, coming into the kitchen and adding a soupçon of sugar to the soup or a pinch of salt to the cake mix. And it is my exhortation, too.

SERVES 8–10

45g butter
60g caster sugar
220g walnut halves
2 tablespoons brandy,
    plus an extra splash
grated zest of 1 orange
grated zest of 1 lime
2 tablespoons maple syrup
2 tablespoons double cream
½ teaspoon orange blossom water
½ teaspoon lemon or lime juice
a tiny pinch of salt
6 Medjool dates, cut into
    thick slivers

For the pastry:
125g plain flour
55g icing sugar
55g chilled unsalted butter
½ beaten egg

For the brûlée topping:
5 egg yolks
100g caster sugar
450ml double cream

First make the pastry. Sift the flour and icing sugar into a bowl and rub in the butter until the mixture resembles breadcrumbs. Mix in the beaten egg until the pastry holds together in a soft ball. Wrap in cling film and chill for a good 15 minutes.

Preheat the oven to 180°C/Gas Mark 4. Butter and flour a 26cm loose-bottomed tart tin. On a lightly floured surface, roll out the pastry to fit the tin – you should have a small lump, the size of a child's fist, left over, which will be useful for patching up any cracks that appear in the pastry after you've baked it. Cover the pastry with greaseproof paper and fill with baking beans or rice. Bake blind for 10 minutes, then carefully remove the paper and beans and return to the oven for 5 minutes. Remove from the oven and leave to cool. Reduce the oven temperature to 110°C/Gas Mark ¼.

To make the filling, melt the butter and sugar in a frying pan till they start to bubble gently and turn a soft golden colour. Add the walnuts and fry for 4–5 minutes, then add the brandy, orange and lime zest, maple syrup and cream. Cook, stirring all the time on a gentle heat, for 5 minutes or so, until the mixture starts to turn into a thick and gently fudgy sauce. Stir in the orange blossom water, lemon or lime juice, salt and an extra splash of brandy. Set aside while you make the brûlée topping.

Using an electric beater, whisk the egg yolks with the caster sugar until thick and creamy and at least doubled in volume. Heat the double cream in a small saucepan until a few bubbles start to break the surface. Pour the hot cream into the egg and sugar mixture, whisking constantly with the beater on a low speed.

If there are any cracks in the pastry case carefully fill them with the reserved pastry – it's especially important to do this around the edge, so that the custard doesn't leak. Now transfer the nuts in their sauce to the pastry case and place it on a baking sheet. Open the oven door and partly pull out the middle shelf. Place the baking sheet on it and carefully pour or ladle the custard over the filling. Push the shelf back into the oven. Bake for 25–30 minutes, till the custard is set but still pale, with a slightly foamy-looking top. Allow to cool, then serve with a small heap of Medjool dates over each portion. The tart keeps for at least 3 days in the fridge.

Peach Tarts with Elderflower Ice Cream

One of the things I've missed most living in Australia is elderflower cordial. I adore it served very cold in sparkling mineral water – sometimes, at the request of my seven-year-old, with a soupçon of rosewater added. In fact it is occasionally available from a few select delis and providores and, though it isn't my aim to send you scurrying there, the IKEA food hall. Now how's that for democracy?

I also make an easy and voluptuous fool with it, served with chocolate pecan thins, which are simply melted dark chocolate into which you've stirred some roughly chopped, lightly toasted pecans, spread into 8cm circles on baking parchment and refrigerated until cold and crisp. If you feel like making the ice cream but not the tarts, I suggest one each of these thins with it.

SERVES 4
150g puff pastry
4 perfectly ripe peaches
icing sugar for dusting

For the elderflower ice cream:
400ml milk
500ml double cream
1 vanilla pod, split open lengthways
 and seeds extracted
8 egg yolks
200g caster sugar
200ml elderflower cordial
a tiny pinch of black pepper

To make the ice cream, put the milk and cream in a saucepan and add the vanilla seeds and pod. Bring to the boil and immediately remove from the heat.

In a bowl, lightly whisk the egg yolks with the caster sugar, then slowly pour half the hot milk and cream on to them, whisking constantly until well amalgamated. Add the remaining cream and milk, transfer to a clean pan and cook very gently, stirring constantly, until the mixture thickens. Half fill a sink with cold water and place the pan in the water to cool. Then add the elderflower cordial and black pepper and transfer to an ice-cream maker. Freeze according to the manufacturer's instructions.

For the tarts, preheat the oven to 220°C/Gas Mark 7. Roll out the pastry to 2mm thick and cut out 4 circles, about 15cm in diameter. Prick the pastry circles all over with a fork, leaving a 1cm rim all the way round so the sides puff up but the centres don't. Stone the peaches and slice them finely. Fan each one out on top of a pastry circle, dust with icing sugar and bake for 15–20 minutes, until caramelised to a rich golden colour. Leave to cool on a wire rack, but serve while still warm, with a scoop of the ice cream.

Nougat with Raspberries, Frangelico, Vanilla Ice Cream and Chantilly Cream

This is a classic nougat, or what Italians sometimes call *torroncini*, a word with a gorgeous ring to it if ever I heard one. I had a version of this dessert in a Byron Bay restaurant with my friend Eve, at the end of too large a meal. Somehow we found room and managed to enjoy it. As one does. Mind you, we went and danced our heads off until midnight afterwards.

I've loved nougat since I was a child, so went to the bother (not that great, as it happens) of making my own for this recipe. But a good-quality Italian or French bought one will do the trick. And there is a good Australian nougat made with macadamias.

SERVES 6
315g caster sugar
150ml liquid glucose
50ml clear, fragrant honey
1 egg white
300g blanched almonds, toasted in a
    dry frying pan until golden brown

For the Chantilly cream:
150ml whipping cream
1 tablespoon icing sugar

For the raspberry layer:
300g fresh or frozen raspberries
150ml Frangelico (or Amaretto) liqueur
300ml good-quality vanilla ice cream

Put the sugar, glucose and honey in a small saucepan and place over a medium heat until the mixture is warm and the sugar begins to dissolve. Turn the heat up and boil for about 7 minutes to allow the flavours to develop; it should look thick and slightly fudgy. Don't be tempted to taste it at this stage, as it will be lethally hot.

With an electric mixer, whisk the egg white in a large bowl until stiff, then add the sugar syrup to it in a thin, steady stream, beating constantly – at first at low speed, then faster – until completely incorporated. Beat for a further minute until the mixture is very thick. Don't be alarmed by the candy floss thread that can form around the beater and the edges of the bowl. Fold in the almonds and mix well with a spoon. Scrape out the mixture on to a very lightly oiled worktop or a piece of baking parchment and flatten to a rough circle about 18cm in diameter and 2cm high. Cover with cling film (or rice paper – see below) and leave in a dry place for about 8 hours to cool and set.

For the Chantilly cream, whip the cream until it forms soft peaks, then fold in the icing sugar.

To assemble, break up the nougat into rough lumps (you probably won't need all of it) and place a piece in each sundae glass. Top with the raspberries, Frangelico, a scoop of ice cream and finally a dollop of Chantilly. Serve at once.

Note

A whole cake of nougat makes a great gift, and at a small fraction of the cost of buying one ready made. If you want to keep the nougat rather than using it in the dessert above, then after you have shaped it into a round, press a sheet of rice paper on to first one and then the other side. Set aside in a dry place for 8 hours, remembering that heat, air and humidity are the enemies of nougat. Store in an airtight tin in a cool cupboard and never in the fridge, where it will just go sticky and gooey.

Caramelised Kumquats

This makes a good alternative to the Frangelico cream and hazelnut praline to serve with the Chocolate Hazelnut Cake on page 168. Sometimes I like to gild the kumquats and the cake with a little gold leaf, if only because I have the words 'Isn't all action prompted by beauty?' on my bedroom wall.

SERVES 4–6

500g kumquats, cut in half,
   pips removed
100ml warm water
2 tablespoons brandy
2 tablespoons orange juice
1 tablespoon soft brown sugar
1 teaspoon orange blossom water

Place the kumquats, water, brandy, orange juice and sugar in a pan and simmer gently for 7–8 minutes, until the kumquats are soft but still holding their own pretty shape, their luminous orange colour, and their one-off topsy-turvy taste, sweet without, sour within. Add a little more water or orange juice during cooking to stop them sticking if necessary, though you should know that this is more like jam than anything else, sticky and densely flavoured. Remove from the heat and stir in the orange blossom water. Serve warm or cold with the chocolate cake, plus some crème fraîche, a little grated orange zest and some gold leaf, if you like.

Almond and Rosewater Cigars

These are a traditional teatime speciality in my family. They are sticky and syrupy, sweet of course, but surprisingly light and crisp, with a lingering note of rose. Do not be tempted to use commercial ground almonds (almond meal), which will be far too clumpy for this delicate recipe.

MAKES 30

250g blanched almonds
120g caster sugar
3 tablespoons rosewater
6 sheets filo pastry
90g unsalted butter, melted
1 litre sunflower oil for deep-frying

For the sugar syrup:
300g caster sugar
300ml water
2 tablespoons rosewater, or to taste
2 cardamom pods, lightly crushed
  (optional)

First prepare the syrup. Put the sugar and water in a pan and heat gently, stirring occasionally, until the sugar has dissolved. Raise the heat and boil, without stirring, until the mixture is thick and syrupy. Remove from the heat and add the rosewater, plus the cardamom pods if using. Set aside.

Put the almonds in a food processor and grind to a mixture of fine and coarser grits. Turn into a bowl and mix with the sugar and rosewater, bringing the mixture together with your hand so it holds into a rough paste. Make 30 thin little sausage shapes out of the mix, bringing your fingers into the palm of your hand over and over until the mixture holds together well. Place on a plate and set aside.

Unroll the filo and turn the sheets of pastry so that the long side is nearest you. Cut the sheets across their width into strips about 8–10cm wide and pile them on top of each other. Cover with a damp tea towel so they do not dry out. Take out one strip at a time and brush with melted butter, leaving a 1cm-wide edge on both sides. Place an almond sausage at one end of the pastry strip, then roll tightly into a 'cigar', making sure the end is well sealed and sticking it down with a little more melted butter or a drop of water, if necessary.

Deep-fry the cigars in hot oil for about 1 minute, until golden, turning them over with 2 forks to make sure they are evenly cooked, and taking care to adjust the heat so the oil doesn't get too hot. Transfer to a plate well lined with absorbent kitchen paper, then to a festive plate, one row piled on top of another, each row at right angles to the row below, till they're all used up – about 7 levels high, with fewer and fewer on each level. This is the precarious and entirely traditional way of serving these and I wouldn't dream of doing it any other way. In fact, to add glamour to ceremony, I use a lipped pedestal plate. Pour the sugar syrup over while both are still hot and carry carefully to the table.

Note

Pouring the hot syrup over the hot cigars will help them stay crisp. Eat soon, though if you accept a loss of crispness they can be kept, covered, in the fridge for several days.

If you want to make a proper dessert of these, you can serve them with a rose and cardamom ice cream, or just a rose-scented whipped cream with a few crystallised rose petals (see page 174) scattered over for prettiness.

Variation: Medjool Dates with Home-made Marzipan
Dipped in Molten Dark Chocolate

This is a made-up extravagance I came up with at the last minute during a cookery class.
Take a dozen Medjool dates, slice them open and remove the stone. Stuff with the same
filling as the cigars and press them closed again.

Melt 100g very dark chocolate in a bowl set over a pan of boiling water. Dip the filled
dates, held on a cocktail stick, into the chocolate, swirling to cover all over. Serve at once
with coffee or, in my case, a large glass of fizzy water.

Frozen Pistachio Halva with Cardamom and Orange Blossom Poached Apricots and Pistachio Glass Biscuits

It happens sometimes, doesn't it? You throw something together in 5 minutes without thinking and you create a masterpiece. Well, I exaggerate, but this is amazing, intriguing and weirdly wonderful. And you need very small portions, as it's so rich. I live in a small town but I've lost track of the times I've been stopped in the street by someone who's made it at home after a cookery class and loved it. It is so ridiculously easy that it's absolutely and completely foolproof.

SERVES 8–12

450g good-quality pistachio halva, with plenty of whole nut through it
100g Greek yoghurt
1 tablespoon icing sugar
grated zest of 1 brightly skinned orange or mandarin
2 teaspoons orange blossom water
300ml double cream

For the poached apricots:
250g soft dried apricots
2 tablespoons orange blossom water
seeds of 3–4 cardamom pods
1 tablespoon soft brown sugar

For the pistachio glass biscuits:
125g pistachio nuts
50g unsalted butter
90g caster sugar
½ teaspoon vanilla extract
45ml liquid glucose
45g plain flour, sifted

Line a 500g loaf tin with cling film, leaving the ends overhanging the tin. Mash the halva and Greek yoghurt together thoroughly with a fork, then mix in the icing sugar, orange zest and orange blossom water. In a separate bowl, lightly whip the cream. Fold it into the halva mixture. Pour into the lined tin, covering with the extra cling film, and freeze overnight.

Place all the ingredients for the poached apricots in a pan, add enough water to cover and bring to the boil. Simmer gently for about 20 minutes, until the apricots are soft and bright and glistening in a generous syrup. Remove from the heat and set aside. For the glass biscuits, preheat the oven to its lowest setting. Spread the pistachios out on a baking tray, place in the oven and leave for about 20 minutes; they shouldn't colour. Skin them by rubbing them in a clean tea towel, then chop roughly.

Increase the oven temperature to 160°C/Gas Mark 3. In a small saucepan over a very gentle heat, melt the butter with the sugar, vanilla and glucose, stirring constantly. Transfer to a bowl and add the flour and pistachios. Stir until the mixture comes together into a dough, then leave to cool.

Shape the cooled mixture into marble-sized balls, about 2.5cm in diameter. Place them on a greased baking tray, leaving a 4–5cm gap between each one to give them space to spread. Bake for 10 minutes; the mixture will spread like brandy snaps and will be golden and somewhat misshapen when done. If you want perfect rounds, apply a biscuit cutter while the biscuits are still hot. Leave to cool on the baking tray for a few minutes, then lift the biscuits off carefully and store in an airtight container until required.

To serve, turn the frozen halva out on to a large, chilled, festive-looking plate and spoon a little of the apricot mixture over and around it. Place the remaining apricots in a small bowl. Cut the halva into thin slices, not more than a finger thick (it is very rich) and place each one on a dessert plate with a spoonful of poached apricots beside it. Serve with the glass biscuits.

White Chocolate Crème Brûlée with Wattle Seeds and Pistachio and Wattle Seed Thins

I probably make crème brûlée more than any other dessert and have finally, after years of resistance, come round to brûlées with a little something extra to them. This one is an adaptation of a recipe from a pull-out supplement that came with *Cosmopolitan* magazine. The wattle seeds are an excuse for using this rare and exclusively Australian ingredient but you can substitute coffee granules to similar effect.

A great tip from that same article suggests that you surround the ramekins with ice cubes before placing them under the grill, to maintain the desirable chill of the brûlées while reaching the heat required to caramelise the sugar.

SERVES 6
600ml double cream
60g caster sugar
1 tablespoon wattle seeds (optional)
150g good-quality white chocolate, broken up into pieces
4 extra-large egg yolks
60g soft brown sugar

For the pistachio and wattle seed thins:
3 egg whites
95g caster sugar
95g plain flour, sifted
100g pistachio nuts
1 tablespoon ground wattle seeds

For the pistachio and wattle seed thins, preheat the oven to 180°C/Gas Mark 4. Line a 450g loaf tin with greaseproof paper or baking parchment and butter lightly. Whisk the egg whites until stiff, then whisk in the sugar a tablespoon at a time. Lightly fold in the flour, nuts and ground wattle seeds to make a soft, sponge-like mixture. Pour into the loaf tin, smooth the top and bake for about 40 minutes, until firm and golden. Turn out on to a wire rack, peel off the baking paper and leave to cool. Reduce the oven temperature to 140°C/Gas Mark 1.

When the loaf is cool enough to handle, slice it as thinly as possible with a very sharp knife and lay the slices on 2 pieces of baking parchment. You should get at least 30 slices. Return to the oven for 6–10 minutes, until they are a very pale golden colour. Remove from the oven and carefully transfer the thins to a wire rack to cool (a palette knife helps to lift them off the paper). They will crisp as they cool. Store in an airtight container until you are ready to use them.

For the brûlée, combine the cream, sugar and wattle seeds, if using, in a bowl set over a pan of simmering water, making sure the water doesn't touch the base of the bowl. Stir until the sugar dissolves, then add the chocolate and stir until melted. Cool slightly.

Use an electric mixer to beat the egg yolks until they are doubled in volume – about 5 minutes. Fold into the chocolate mixture and pour into six 150ml ramekins or equivalent ovenproof dishes. Place in a baking tray and pour in enough hot water to come half way up the sides of the ramekins. Bake at 140°C/Gas Mark 1 for 50–60 minutes, until set. Remove from the tray and allow to cool. Cover with cling film and chill for at least 3 hours.

Just before serving, sprinkle the brown sugar over the ramekins and place under a preheated hot grill (or use a blowtorch) so that the sugar caramelises. Serve immediately.

Russian Soured Cream Cake

I was given the recipe for something like this 23 years ago, by someone I have long since lost touch with. I didn't write the recipe down but made it often over a two-year period while running the kitchen of a North London restaurant. Since then, my memory of it has been a little vague, soured cream and layered fried pastry being the most salient details. Then, some time ago, I came across a recipe for sweet pirozhky (individual crescent-shaped cheese-filled pastries) in *delicious* magazine and I had an idea that we might be alluding to a similar thing. So I played around with the pastry, using a little less butter, a little more soured cream than the magazine recipe suggested, and came back quite easily to the cake of my memory. The pastry is very delicate, friable and fragile. Don't worry if the cooked sheets crack as you lift them. It'll all patch up with the filling.

SERVES 6–8
200ml soured cream
200g mascarpone cheese
5 tablespoons caster sugar
100g big, fat, juicy raisins
1 tablespoon lemon juice
100ml sunflower oil for frying
icing sugar for dusting

For the pastry:
225g plain flour
a pinch of salt
125g unsalted butter,
    cut into cubes
1 egg
2 tablespoons soured cream

To serve:
100g raisins
grated zest of 1 lemon
1 tablespoon lemon juice
1 tablespoon caster sugar
2 tablespoons vodka

To make the pastry, place the flour, salt and butter in a food processor and process to fine crumbs. Add the egg and soured cream and blitz again until the mixture is soft and smooth. Wrap in cling film and chill for at least 30 minutes, or overnight if it's easier. Roll out the pastry on a lightly floured surface to a thickness of 3mm. Using a dessert plate as a template, cut out five 19–20cm circles from the pastry. Lift carefully by sliding 2 fish slices under each one or – my failsafe piece of kitchen wizardry – the well-floured loose base of a metal tart tin. Place a dinner plate upside down over it and flip back the right way round so that the pastry lands flat on the plate. Frankly, it helps to slide each piece of pastry on to a different plate, but that assumes plenty of fridge space or a knack for fitting things in one way or the other. Otherwise, carefully stack one piece on top of the other with a piece of baking parchment in between and refrigerate for 30 minutes.

Meanwhile, make the filling. Mix the soured cream, mascarpone, caster sugar, raisins and lemon juice together, giving them a good stir so that they stiffen up a little (but not too much, so go easy). Set aside.

Heat a couple of tablespoons of the sunflower oil in a frying pan and fry the sheets of pastry over a medium heat, one at a time, for about 1½ minutes per side. Don't be tempted to lift the pastry before that. Transfer to a wire rack to cool. Clean the pan in between each one, using plenty of kitchen paper and adding more oil each time.

Place the raisins, lemon zest and juice, sugar and vodka in a small pan and bring to the boil. Reduce the heat and simmer for 5 minutes (you can prepare this in advance if you like).

To serve, transfer one sheet of pastry to a plate and spread with a quarter of the filling, then slide another piece on top. Continue in this careful way until all the pastry and filling are used up, ending with a pastry layer. Dust with icing sugar and serve the warm vodka and lemon raisins by the side, with a decorative mound on top.

Chocolate Macaroons

Every time my brother returns from Paris, he brings back a beribboned box of gooey, pastel- and chocolate-coloured macaroons, held together with gorgeous chocolate cream. In fact, when I went to Paris with my son recently, 'Eat macaroons' was at the top of my list, above 'Visit Eiffel Tower' and 'Go to the Louvre'.

I had already handed in the text for this book but it didn't take much persuading to get this recipe included. The macaroons are very easy to make and only take a short while to cook, so I hope you'll make them often. You could divide the mixture into three, reduce the cocoa powder accordingly and flavour the other two parts with ½ teaspoon of raspberry essence and a few drops of red food colouring, and pistachio essence and a little green food colouring respectively.

MAKES ABOUT 36
225g icing sugar
125g ground almonds (almond meal)
2½ tablespoons cocoa powder
4 egg whites
2 tablespoons caster sugar
2 teaspoons cornflour

For the filling:
200g good-quality dark chocolate, finely chopped
100ml double cream

Sift the icing sugar into a bowl and then sift again with the ground almonds (almond meal) and cocoa powder. Set aside.

Using a mixer on high speed, whisk the egg whites until firm. Add the caster sugar and cornflour and continue whisking until they form stiff peaks. Gently but thoroughly fold in the almond, sugar and cocoa mixture with a spatula or metal spoon – not a wooden spoon, which would flatten the mix.

Use a teaspoon and your finger to scoop out small amounts of the mixture, 2cm in diameter, on to baking trays lined with baking parchment, placing them 2.5cm apart. Bake for 12–15 minutes, until the macaroons are risen, smooth, rounded and glossy on top with a thin, crisp, biscuity base. Leave to cool and don't attempt to lift them off the paper till completely cold.

Meanwhile, put the chocolate in a heatproof bowl over a pan of boiling water and bring the cream to the boil in a separate pan. When the chocolate has melted, pour the cream into it and stir till smooth and shiny. Allow to cool completely. Sandwich the macaroons together with the chocolate cream and serve.

The macaroons can be stored in an airtight tin. However, if you leave them out too long and they dry out, put them in an airtight container with a piece of bread. By the next day, the macaroons will be soft again and the bread dry as toast!

Index

Bibliography

Abensur, Nadine (2004), *The Cranks Bible*, London: Orion

Alexander, Stephanie (1998), *The Cook's Companion*, Sydney: Viking

Johnson, Philip (2002), *E'cco 2*, Sydney: Random House

Malouf, Greg and Lucy (2001), *Moorish*, Prahran: Hardie Grant Publishing

Owen, Sri (1994), *Indonesian Regional Food and Cookery*, London: Doubleday

Roden, Claudia (1999), *The Book of Jewish Food*, Sydney: Viking

Thompson, David (2002), *Thai Food*, Sydney: Viking

Roux, Michel and Albert, (1986), *The Roux Brothers on Patisserie*,
London: Little Brown

Acknowledgements

I would like to thank my publisher Denise Bates at Collins UK for taking on
this book and working on it with me from the other side of the world, an act
of faith even in these days of emails and modern technology. I thoroughly enjoyed
our conversations across time zones. I would also like to thank Julie Gibbs of
Penguin Australia for believing in the book and taking the unusual step of
jointly publishing it.

I would also like to thank Jane Middleton for her fine toothcomb editing.
It was a pleasure to work with her and I hope our paths cross again. And I would
like to thank designers Smith & Gilmour for making the book so beautiful
and easy to negotiate.